NEW YORK'S 50 BEST

—

Wonderful Things to Do at the Holidays

BY
M@NI📞ttoⁿ
USER'S GUIDE

Illustrations by Chesley McLaren

CITY & COMPANY
New York

First Edition
Printed in the United States of America
ISBN 1-885492-43-X

Library of Congress Cataloging-in-Publication Data is available upon request.

PUBLISHER'S NOTE:
Neither City & Company nor the author has any interest, financial or personal, in the locations listed in this book. No fees were paid or services rendered in exchange for inclusion in these pages. Please call ahead for up-to-date fees and hours. All area codes are 212 unless otherwise noted.

Special editions of City & Company books can be created to specification. Contact the Sales Director at the address below.

City & Company
22 West 23rd Street
New York, NY 10010

Contents

Introduction

WHEN WE SAT DOWN TO WRITE THIS BOOK, we knew we would include the hallmarks of the holidays in New York: the snowflake on Fifth Avenue, the tree at Rockefeller Center, the performance of the Messiah at St. John the Divine, the Macy's Thanksgiving Day parade, Times Square on New Year's Eve, the department store windows, gift shopping, and where to have a holiday meal.

Then, as it always does, New York surprised us: how the United Nations created a *Nutcracker* prince; the story of the 300 tubas; what the Salvation Army does every year at the "21" Club; what prompted Alfred Polizzotto of Bensonhurst to give out 250,000 candy canes on his front lawn; a secret source for collectible Christopher Radko ornaments; the one place in New York on New Year's Eve where you can hear the Brandenburg Concertos, have Champagne, see the skyline of Manhattan, *and* watch fireworks.

Written for both residents and visitors, we hope this book will encourage you to explore some of New York's well-known traditions as well as some of the more hidden treasures. There are more than 50 things to do in this book, but that's New York for you.

Arrival of the Season

*I*T'S LATE AFTERNOON IN DECEMBER and you probably fall into one of two categories: you're either caught
up in the holiday spirit and you'd like to get out and enjoy
the city or, you couldn't be less in the holiday spirit, but at
least a tiny part of you would like to be. Walk this way.

Get your ebullient (or cranky) self to the plaza in front of the
Plaza Hotel, Fifth Ave. and 59th St. From there you get to
look at the horse-drawn carriages, F.A.O. Schwarz, the
Plaza itself, Central Park. Buy some hot chestnuts and
watch the crowds.

Stop by ***Barnes and Noble,*** 600 Fifth Ave. [48th] 765-0590, at
Rockefeller Center, and treat yourself to something you've
been wanting to curl up with.

See what ***Saks,*** 611 Fifth Ave. [49th/50th] 753-4000, has in
their windows and step inside if you're susceptible, as we
are, to department store buzz. Get an extra gift for someone on your list.

Cross Fifth Avenue to the ***Channel Gardens*** down toward
the ice skating rink at Rockefeller Center. Every New
Yorker (and visitor) should spend a few minutes of the hol-

iday season leaning over the railing, looking down at the skaters and up at the tree, just because it's such a pleasure.

Walk east to Park Avenue, enjoying the great street at its most festive. You'll see the **Park Avenue Memorial Trees** that run from 54th Street up to 96th and many other holiday effects, courtesy of the various companies and building owners.

Pass through the **Helmsley Building**, 230 Park Ave. [46th], arcade on your way to Grand Central. The beautiful station is in the midst of a renovation, but there should be some holiday activities and music to enjoy.

We never miss a chance to step into one of the city's most civilized places, the **Pierpont Morgan Library,** 29 E. 36th St. [Madison/Park] 685-0610, where, in addition to Mr. Morgan's glorious library and study, there are always exhibits worth seeing.

Now we're ready for a tiny libation, so we'd nip into **Molly's,** 287 Third Ave. [22nd/23rd] 889-3361, a most pleasant Irish pub, for a pint of Guinness and to warm up by the wood-burning fireplace.

There's no more Russian Tea Room with its year-round Christmas decorations, but there is **Rolf's,** 281 Third Ave. [22nd] 477-4750, festooned with lights and all the holiday trimmings. When the days start to get dark early, stop in for some hearty German food.

That should have enhanced or improved your holiday mood. If not, read on.

Buildings with Decorations

𝒩EW YORK DRESSES UP FOR THE HOLIDAYS. You'll find ribbons, lights, wreaths, toy soldiers, menorahs, ornaments, stars, angels, Santas, elves, and crèches, in lobbies, on facades, on rooftops, in hallways and elevators. A few highlights:

EMPIRE STATE BUILDING: The lobby of the Empire State Building, 350 Fifth Ave. [33rd/34th], is treed and wreathed. There is a menorah during Hanukkah and the Star and Crescent. Enter the building by the Fifth Avenue entrance and you will find the windows called The Fifth Avenue Gallery. They contain Christmas and Hanukkah art exhibits. During the month of December, there is live music Mon.-Fri., 12:30 P.M.-1:30 P.M.

THE LEVER HOUSE: The first carousel in the lobby of Lever House, 390 Park Ave. [53rd], came from Asbury Park and was installed in 1953 as a way to show off the company's cleaning products. Now, a different story is told each year by the swirling figures. Designer Jack Lowery has created the carousel from the early days. If you are near the Lever building in the five days just after Thanksgiving, you can watch his crew assemble it.

NEW YORK PUBLIC LIBRARY: Stop by the New York Public Library, Fifth Ave. and 41st St., 930-0800, to see the large, lighted evergreen wreaths on the necks of the lions named Patience and Fortitude (left and right as you face the library) by Mayor Fiorello LaGuardia. They and you are serenaded by carolers during a fifteen minute ceremony that usually takes place on the first Friday in December at 11:55 A.M. Step inside to see the holiday tree, a menorah, a kinara, and a Star and Crescent in Astor Hall.

STORE WINDOWS: Perennial favorites are the store window displays around town. **Lord & Taylor,** 424 Fifth Ave. [38th/39th] 391-3344, did the first holiday windows anywhere in 1905 and they remain popular, as do the **Saks** windows (see more in the entry on Saks). At **Cartier,** Fifth Ave. and 52nd St. 753-0111, the whole building gets wrapped in a bright red ribbon.

TISHMAN BUILDING: At the Tishman Bldg., 666 Fifth Ave. [52nd/53rd], 40 candles and 16 stars decorate the outside of the building up to the 8th floor. On Thanksgiving, the lights are turned on and stay illuminated until Little Christmas, January 6th.

Buildings with Lights

ONE OF THE PLEASURES OF THE HOLIDAY SEASON in New York is the spectacle of so many illuminated buildings gleaming red, green, and white.

The most famous is, of course, the **Empire State Building,** 350 Fifth Ave. [33rd/34th], which sports red and green lights for the holidays. The top of the building is lit in red and yellow from the weekend after Halloween until the night before the Rockefeller Center tree lighting, when it changes to red and green. Normally the lights go off at midnight, but on December 24th, 25th, and 31st and January 1st, they stay on until 3 A.M. On December 1st, the building is dark for 15 minutes as part of "Day Without Art/Night Without Light" AIDS Awareness.

There are other buildings that make use of holiday colors as well. One is the **Metropolitan Life Tower** building at Madison Ave. and 24th St., the design of which is based on the Campanile of St. Mark's in Venice. The building has been illuminated since 1980.

From December 1st to the beginning of February, the **Con Ed Building,** Irving Plaza and 14th St., changes the lights on the clock, the columned belfry and the lantern to red and green. The building was designed by Warren and Wetmore in 1926.

Other favorites include the **snowflake** hanging over the intersection at Fifth Avenue and 57th Street. It was designed by Douglas Leigh, the lighting designer responsible for many of the city's illuminated buildings.

In the fall, **Tavern on the Green,** Central Park West and 67th St. 873-3200, installs 500,000 little blue lights. During the holidays, it's a Christmas fantasyland with garlands, wreaths, ribbons, and two big Christmas trees. The tree in the Crystal Room has more than 10,000 hand-painted ornaments and the topiary animals get dressed up as well.

The dramatic space of **The Winter Garden,** 1 World Financial Center 945-0505, has appropriately dramatic holiday lighting. Suspended from the 120-foot high ceiling are 32 mirrored discs with 100,000 or so lights hanging down from them. The switch is thrown in early December in a ceremony with local schoolchildren as the guests of honor. Free orchestral and choral concerts take place during the month at noontime, in the evening, and on Sundays. A holiday market with over 80 vendors is installed on the bridge between the World Trade Center and the Winter Garden.

The windows of the **MetLife** building, 200 Park Ave. [45th], are lit to form a large cross.

Downtown, **shooting stars** project from lampposts on Broadway from St. Paul's Chapel to Bowling Green and on Wall and Church Streets.

Carols and Candlelight

W HAT'S KNOWN FOR SURE is that the day was cold, damp, and dreary when either Jack Kriendler or Charlie Berns stepped outside their *"21" Club* for a minute and spotted the Salvation Army Band at the corner of Fifth Ave. and 52nd St.

A "21" tradition was started when the band was invited in to warm up over bowls of soup. The Salvation Army Band has made appearances at the restaurant for over 50 years, leading the diners in a sing-along at a few meals in the weeks before Christmas. After the carols are sung, everyone joins in two songs added to the program by longtime diners at "21," "The Battle Hymn of the Republic," and "Dixie," this last requested by Mrs. Douglas MacArthur, a native of Tennessee. *"21" Club,* 21 W. 52nd St. [5th/6th] 582-7200. Reservations required.

The route changes each year for composer *Phil Kline's caroling party,* but here is how it works. Mr. Kline composes a new Christmas piece each year, a kind of "musical collage" of synthesized music, human voices, and instrumentation with recognizable carols threaded in. He records it in 60 or so parts which are put into 60 boom boxes that are carried by as many participants. The electronic carolers string out for a block or two along a route that always ends in a park. Mr. Kline says, "It's like draping the city with several yards of sound." To be a carrier or a walking listener, call 227-6255. Free.

The Abigail Adams Smith Museum, 421 E. 61st St. [1st/York] 838-6878, recalls the 1830s when the house was the Mount Vernon Hotel, a country escape. The house is decorated for the holidays, and musicians play on the second-floor landing as you are led on a candlelit tour of the period rooms. Tickets required.

The neo-Romanesque *Greek Orthodox Archdiocesan Cathedral of the Holy Trinity,* 319 E. 74th St. [1st/2nd] 704-2100, is candlelit for the annual Christmas concert of the Little Orchestra Society. Tickets required.

The Old Merchant's House, 29 E. 4th St. [Lafayette/Bowery] 777-1089, built in 1832, is a Federal-style house with a Greek revival interior. In December, the house gets full holiday decorations and you can take an evening candlelight tour. Tickets required.

At *Riverside Church,* 490 Riverside Dr. [120th/122th] 870-6700, the candlelight carol festival includes the adult and the children's choirs, a bell choir and instrumentalists. Suggested donation.

In *Washington Square Park* at 5 P.M. on Christmas Eve near the arch, sing carols, usually to a brass band accompaniment. Free.

Join the *West Village Chorale* on their caroling walk. Meet at the Church of St. Luke-in-the-Fields, 487 Hudson St. [Barrow/Grove] 570-7301, where you pick up sheet music and candles, then divide into groups of twenty and take various paths through the West Village.

Clement Clarke Moore

$\sharp \natural$

𝒩EW YORK'S OLDEST CONTINUING HOLIDAY TRADITION
honors Clement Clarke Moore.

That's fitting, since Mr. Moore's poem, "A Visit from
St. Nicholas," did much to popularize the more fanciful
aspects of Christmas. The tradition came about like this: Mr.
Moore was originally buried in the cemetery at St. Luke-
in-the-Fields on Hudson St. in 1863. When the land was
judged too swampy for such a purpose and was sold off, the
bodies were moved and the swamp was filled in and built
over. Mr. Moore was reinterred in the **Trinity Cemetery,**
155th St. and Riverside Drive near the Church of the
Intercession, 555 W. 155th St. [Broadway] 283-6200. The
church began to honor Mr. Moore and to give its own gift to
the children of New York in 1911.

On the fourth Sunday of Advent at 4 P.M., Canon
Frederick B. Williams and Reverend Earl Kooperkamp
hold a service in the church. Guest musicians and the church
choir are backed by Iain Quinn on the Aeolian Skinner
organ. Past guests have included the Harlem Boys Choir,
who had their beginnings here. All the children attending
are invited to come forward and sit in the center of the nave

while a New York celebrity reads "A Visit from St. Nicholas." St. Nicholas himself appears, in the appropriately costumed person of Mr. Henry Tully, a retired postman and congregant, to lead everyone on a procession to Clement Clarke Moore's grave, two blocks away in Trinity Cemetery. Candles on the sidewalk light the path and congregants carry kerosene lanterns. St. Nicholas lays a wreath on Moore's grave, a prayer is said, and everyone sings "Silent Night." A tent on the cemetery grounds holds hot mulled cider and treats for the children.

(See the entry "'Twas the Night Before Christmas.")

Dancing

ℛETURN TO THE NEW YORK OF ANOTHER ERA by spending an evening dining and dancing at the **Rainbow Room**, 30 Rockefeller Plaza [49th/50th] 632-5000, sixty-five floors above it all. If you don't want to make an entire evening of it, you can come just for dancing. In both cases, call ahead.

You can also step out at the following places:
There is dinner and room to tango at **Bistro Latino**, 1711 Broadway [54th] 956-1000.

The **Metropolitan Duane Hall Church**, 201 W. 13th St. [7th] 459-4080, has English country and contra dancing.

Denim & Diamonds, 511 Lexington Ave. [48th] 371-1600, for country and western, line, two-step, and swing dancing to music with a deejay.

Louisiana Community Bar and Grill, 622 Broadway [Bleecker/Houston] 460-9633, features Cajun swing to a live band.

Judy Petardi and Dwight Carter, who were taxi dancers at Roseland, have been holding dances in the **Marc Ballroom,** 27 Union Sq. W. [16th/17th] 867-3789, every other Sunday night for more than a decade. Deejayed music.

Dance to a small band on weekends at **Maxim's,** 680 Madison Ave. [61st/62nd] 751-5111.

The New York Swing Dance Society, 696-9737, holds dances at Irving Plaza, 17 Irving Place [15th], most Sunday nights with live music.

Swing West Coast style at the **North River Bar,** 145 Hudson St. [Hubert/Beach] 226-9411. Deejayed music.

You can still begin the beguine at **Roseland Ballroom,** 239 W. 52nd St. [Broadway/8th] 247-0200. They feature a variety of musical styles, depending on the night.

Samba the night away to live Brazilian bands at **S.O.B.'s,** 200 Varick St. [W. Houston] 243-4940.

On some nights, the **Supper Club,** 240 W. 47th St. [Broadway/8th] 921-1940, has a swing orchestra.

Doing Good

*F*OOD, CLOTHING AND YOUR TIME are some of the things you can offer the needy. Here are several ways.

The post office does a few things right. One of them is at the holidays, when letters addressed to "Santa Claus, North Pole" get routed to the *J. A. Farley General Post Office,* Eighth Ave. and 33rd St. 967-8585. Sorted by location of the sender, they are put out in boxes on the main floor. You can then play Santa Claus to your heart's content and a child's delight. If you can't get to the post office, the telephone operators will help you select a letter.

WNYC's program *New York Kids* (Sunday evenings from 6 to 8 P.M. on 93.9FM) asks for handmade Christmas cards from their listeners. The colorful creations are distributed in the children's wards of city hospitals and in homeless shelters. Send cards to *Holiday Cards, WNYC, New York Kids,* 1 Centre St. New York, NY 10007.

New York Cares, 228-5000, has two special holiday programs. One is the Secret Santa program, in which they pass along letters from children to volunteers who fulfill their wishes. The other is the Holiday Coat Drive. Winter coats for adults and children are collected at hundreds of sites around town. 223-CARE (223-2273) for coat drive info.

At the ***Mayor's Voluntary Action Center,*** 788-7550, there is always a need for mentors and tutors to work with teens, for people to give support to those with AIDS, and for people to visit the elderly. During the holidays, they need one-day volunteers to serve meals.

The ***Volunteer Referral Center,*** 745-8249, refers volunteers to not-for-profit agencies around town. While there are a lot of people who want to give a day or two of time around the holidays, they stress that "it's the day after that counts."

Organizations that work year-round to feed the hungry: The ***Holy Apostles Soup Kitchen,*** 924-0167; ***City Harvest,*** 463-0456; ***Citymeals-on-Wheels,*** 687-1234; and ***God's Love We Deliver,*** 294-8100.

Early in December, the ***Apollo Foundation*** sponsors Toys and Books for Kids. To get into the variety show at the Apollo Theatre, 253 W. 125th St. [8th/Adam Clayton Powell, Jr.] 864-0372, the entrance fee is one new book or toy for a child. The show is made up of known and not-so-known acts in the Apollo tradition. The toys and books are distributed to 10 charities, including Hale House, and to children in hospitals.

Not everyone realizes that the ***Big Apple Circus*** is a not-for-profit organization. A donation to them can send their Clown Care Unit into hospitals or to supply circus tickets to children, seniors or physically challenged people. 268-2500.

Fireplaces

THE TRADITION OF THE YULE LOG has lasted hundreds of years in Europe, though these days, it is likely to be in the form of the French *bûche de Noël* (see more in the entry "Foods—International"). In olden days, a large log would be cut on Christmas Eve and brought ceremoniously into the home. Oil, salt, and wine were then poured on it, and a piece of wood, saved from the previous year's log, was used to light the new one.

There is a wide range of restaurants and bars in the city that, while they don't necessarily carry on the tradition of the Yule log, do offer the warmth and cheer of a fireplace.

RESTAURANTS

Chelsea Bistro and Bar, 358 W. 23rd St. [8th/9th] 727-2026

Christer's, 145 W. 55th St. [6th/7th] 974-4449

Chumley's, 86 Bedford St. [Grove/Barrow] 675-4449

Cornelia St. Cafe, 29 Cornelia St. [W. 4th] 989-9319

Demi, 1316 Madison Ave. [93rd] 534-3475

Friend of a Farmer, 77 Irving Pl. [18th/19th] 477-2188

I Trulli , 122 E. 27th St. [Park Ave. So./Lexington] 481-7372

Keens, 72 W. 36th St. [5th/6th] 947-3636

March, 405 E. 58th St. [1st/Sutton Pl.] 754-6272

Marylou's, 21 W. 9th St. [5th/6th] 533-0012

Mary's, 42 Bedford St. [Leroy] 741-3387

Paris Commune, 411 Bleecker St. [Bank/W. 11th] 929-0509

Pierre au Tunnel, 250 W. 47th St. [Broadway/8th] 575-1220

Rene Pujol, 321 W. 51st St. [8th/9th] 246-3023

Restaurant Raphael, 33 W. 54th St. [5th/6th] 582-8993

Santa Fe, 72 W. 69th St. [Columbus/CPW] 724-0822

Savoy, 70 Prince St. [Crosby] 219-8570

Vivolo, 140 E. 74th St. [Lexington/Park] 737-3533

Water Club, 500 E. 30th St. [East River] 683-3333

Ye Waverly Inn, 16 Bank St. [Greenwich] 929-4377

BARS

All State Cafe, 250 W. 72nd St. [Broadway/West End] 874-1883; **Beekman Bar and Books,** 889 First Ave. [50th] 980-9314; **Merchants NY,** 1125 First Ave. [62nd] 832-1551, 521 Columbus Ave. [85th/86th] 721-3689, 112 Seventh Ave. [16th/17th] 366-7267; **"21" Club,** 21 W. 52nd St. [5th/6th] 582-7200

Foods - International

$\mathcal{N}$EW YORK IS BOTH A MELTING POT and a place where traditions from around the world are proudly upheld. At holiday time, you can sample all kinds of international food specialties, re-created for local consumption.

BRITISH: **Myers of Keswick,** 634 Hudson St. [Horatio/Jane] 691-4914, for Christmas puddings and cakes, tiny mince pies, Cumberland sausages, and holiday teas.

FRENCH: **Marquet Patisserie,** 15 E. 12th St. [5th/University] 229-9313, has the quintessential *bûche de Noël*. This is the Christmas dessert of Genoese sponge cake and butter cream made to look like a Yule log.

GERMAN: **Stork's Pastry Shop,** 12-42 150th St. Whitestone 718-767-9220, is unbeatable for gingerbread houses and *pfeffernüsse* (spiced cookies in the shape of a ball), *spekulatius* (spiced biscuits), and *lebkuchen* (gingerbread cookies).

GREEK: On January 1st, a round bread called *vasilopita* is eaten. A coin baked inside the loaf is supposed to bring good luck to the person who gets it in their slice. **Poseidon Bakery,** 629 Ninth Ave. [44th/45th] 757-6173, sells it.

HUNGARIAN: A *bagjal* is a cake filled with either poppy

seeds or walnuts. You will find it at **Tibor Meat,** 1508 Second Ave. [78th/79th] 744-8292.

IRISH: Heavy, dark fruitcakes are the holiday specialty. Called porter cakes if the fruit has been soaked in Guinness or Murphy's and whiskey cakes if the fruit has been soaked in fine *usque baugh* (Irish whiskey), they're to be found at **Mattie Haskin's Shamrock Imports,** 901 Ave. of the Americas [35th] 4th level, 564-7474.

ITALIAN: **DeRobertis,** 176 First Ave. [10th/11th] 674-7137, has the traditional egg, prosciutto and mozzarella pie known as *rustica.*

MEXICAN: On January 6th, Mexicans celebrate with a *rosca de reyes.* This is a sweet bread with dried fruit on top that contains a tiny, plastic baby doll. The person who gets the doll in their slice of *rosca* has to organize a party on February 2nd. *Roscas* are available at **Mexico Pequeño,** 157 Allen St. [Stanton/Rivington] 254-4914.

POLISH: On Christmas Eve, families gather for a traditional multicourse meal. The all-important dried Polish mushrooms can be purchased at **Kurowycky Meats,** 124 First Ave. [7th/8th] 477-0344.

SCANDINAVIAN: Lucia Buns, sweet buns flavored with saffron, are the essential food for the Santa Lucia Day celebrations. You will find them at **Nordic Delicacies,** 6909 Third Ave. [Bay Ridge Ave.] Brooklyn 718-748-1874.

UKRAINIAN: **The Ukrainian Museum,** 203 Second Ave. [12th/13th] 228-0110, sells *medivnyk,* a traditional honey bread, and *makivynk,* a poppy seed bread containing nuts and raisins, at their annual bazaar in early December.

Foods - Prepared

WHEN YOU DON'T FEEL LIKE PREPARING holiday meals yourself, there are plenty of takeout shops and catering companies that are happy to step up to the plate.

Charlotte's Catering, 732-7939, is not only an excellent caterer but an exceptionally nice group to boot.

City Bakery, 22 E. 17th St. [Broadway/5th] 366-1414. Maury Rubin's tarts, pies, and other sweet things are, we warn you, highly addictive. They're great for holiday desserts.

The Cleaver Co., Chelsea Market, 75 Ninth Ave. [15th/16th] 741-9174. Mary Cleaver's company will do everything from finding a location for your party (if you don't want to use your home) to providing decorations, entertainment, staffing, and food.

Colette Peters, the well-known cakemaker, creates gingerbread houses for the holidays. You can even give her a photo of a house you'd like her to turn into gingerbread. 366-6530.

Flavors, 8 W. 18th St. [5th/6th] 647-1234. You can walk in any day and find some of the very best takeout food in the city. At the holidays, there are special menus to make holiday entertaining easier. They do full-service catering as well.

Good and Plenty to Go, 410 W. 43rd St. [9th/10th] 268-4385, does a fine job of preparing foods to take out and also caters parties and events. You can get terrific pies from *The Little Pie Co.,* 424 W. 43rd St. [9th/10th] 736-4780, next door.

Manna, 24 Harrison St. [Hudson/Greenwich] 966-3449, a Kosher caterer, will supply the food for a Hanukkah get-together of 10 or more people. Their specialty at this time of year is 'latkes from around the world' so guests can sample the variations on this favorite dish from international Jewish communities.

Parties by Rossi, 463-0872. Chef Rossi has been catering parties for over 10 years. She does many small parties in people's homes as well as larger events, and she specializes in American regional cuisine.

Spoonbread Catering, 734-0430. Norma Darden, and her sister Carole, run this operation that serves tasty food, some of it with their southern flair, as well as African, West Indian, Latin, and other national and ethnic specialties.

Word of Mouth, 1012 Lexington Ave. [72nd] 734-9483. For quality take-home food, Word of Mouth fills the bill. They are also a full service caterer.

Hanukkah

$\mathcal{H}$ANUKKAH, one of the seven major Jewish holidays, is celebrated for the victory of the Maccabees over the Syrian Greeks around 165 B.C. The Temple of Jerusalem was reconsecrated and the miracle of a day's worth of oil burning for eight is commemorated with the lighting of the candles of the Menorah.

The temple ***Ansche Chesed,*** 251 W. 100th St. [Broadway/Amsterdam] 865-0600, does three things over the Hanukkah holidays. About two weeks ahead, on Saturday night and Sunday, they hold the Hanukkah Arts Festival, the first Judaic fine arts program in New York City. Forty vendors come from the United States and elsewhere selling Judaica and there are storytellers, singers and a puppet/magic show to entertain the children. Also at Hanukkah, popular singer Debbie Friedman performs Jewish folk songs. Tickets required. Finally, there is a family dinner at which latkes, apple sauce, and *susganiot,* a jelly doughnut, are served. Frying the doughnut and latkes in oil is a reminder of the miracle of the oil in the temple.

The ***92nd St. Y,*** 1395 Lexington Ave. [92nd/93rd] 996-1100, has their master storyteller, Peninnah Schram, relate the story of this holiday of liberation in a program for parents and children. Tickets required...Before the holiday, attend a Hanukkah Family Workshop that includes singing and dancing, a presentation of the story, and menorah- and dreidel-making. Registration required...Jewish books and tapes, games, candles, and chocolate coins are among the items for sale at the Y Hanukkah Gift Shop, set up about two weeks before the start of the holiday.

Handcrafted and one-of-a-kind menorahs, tzdukkah boxes, and dreidels can be found at **In The Spirit,** 460 E. 79th St. [1st/York] 861-5222, by appointment. Brenda Bernstein, the owner, highlights the boxes, which is where you put the money you are going to share with others during the season. You will find pottery, hand-carved wood, aluminum, sterling silver and brass items.

Look for more dreidels and menorahs at **Feller's Judaica Gift Gallery,** 1205 Lexington Ave. [81st/82nd] 472-2300, and the gift shop at the **Central Synagogue,** 123 E. 55th St. [Park/Lexington] 833-5122.

The Jewish Museum, 1109 Fifth Ave. [92nd] 423-3230, holds a family holiday program. Tickets required. Their gift shop carries a wide array of menorahs, basic to fancy, affordable to fine art. They also have dreidels and candles, and Hanukkah-related books, tapes and CDs, including many things for children.

There is a large menorah at **59th Street and Fifth Avenue** in front of the Plaza. A lighting ceremony takes place each evening of Hanukkah.

Holiday Drinks

*T*HE CITY DISPENSES PLENTY OF HOLIDAY CHEER from shakers, taps, and bottles all over town.

Ray Deter's bar ***d.b.a.,*** 41 First Ave. [2nd/3rd] 475-5097, attaches their 14 taps to good holiday beers each year. Mr. Deter says, "In England and Europe there is a strong tradition of Christmas beers. The breweries showcase their most interesting beers around this season. In general they are higher in alcohol, and some are spiced." Here are three brews that he thinks represent the best of the tradition. **Snow Goose** is produced by the Wild Goose brewery in Maryland. "It's a traditional English holiday ale. Deep amber in color, it's sublime when available in casks." **Young's Winter Warmer** on draft: "It's not spiced or sweetened, but seems to have more of everything that they put in their beers. . . Many of the Belgian beers are great, but if I have to pick just one it would be **Avec Les Bons Voeux de la Brasserie Dupont.** It comes only in bottles and is so high in alcohol it is almost a wine." d.b.a is one of the most underdecorated bars in town. At Christmas they have a tree decorated by ornaments brought in by customers.

The Greatest Bar on Earth at the World Trade Center, 1 World Trade Center 107th floor 524-7000, on the other hand, is fully decorated year-round and ratchets up a notch for the holidays. Seasonal cocktails are added to their lengthy list of spirits and other offerings.

Drinking one of Dale DeGroff's holiday cocktails in ***The Promenade Bar at the Rainbow Room,*** 30 Rockefeller Plaza 632-5100, looking out on the red and green top of the Empire State Building, is certainly a unique New York high. Mr. DeGroff invents new cocktails (some nonalcoholic) for each holiday season, but there are three that are standards on the Christmas menu. His Rainbow Glögg is a spiced wine with a shot of vodka, his eggnog is a lightened version made with bourbon, and the Holiday Cup is a rum drink with a bit of cinnamon schnapps.

More: While the bar at ***Tavern on the Green,*** Central Park West and 67th St. 873-3200, does not look out into the garden, the sheer over-the-top decoration of the place always makes it feel like Christmas. And you don't need a reservation to sit there. . .***Bar 89,*** 89 Mercer St. [Spring/Broome] 274-0989, with its minimalist downtown look and picture window onto the world of Soho, is a chic spot for a refresher course in martinis. . .***The Mark Bar in the Mark Hotel,*** 25 E. 77th St. [5th/Madison] 744-3400, is an oasis of upholstered civility. Sit back, munch a few of their seasoned nuts, and forget about the shopping list for a few minutes.

House of Lights

𝒯HE WINNER FOR MOST CANDY CANES distributed in a Christmas season? Mr. Alfred Polizzotto of Bensonhurst, who gave out 250,000 in 1996.

Mr. Polizzotto contends that his house at 1145 84th St. [11th/12th] in Brooklyn "is one of the most well known houses in New York," and he's probably right. That's because in the two weeks before Christmas, several hundred thousand folks drop by to see how he's turned his home and property into a mechanized toyland.

"The Nutcracker Suite" is the "nondenominational theme" of the decorations. Wooden soldiers, 27 feet tall, move their arms and feet, and there are two white steeds, each weighing 2,000 pounds, carrying some smaller moving toy soldiers on their backs. Eight dancing dolls of appropriate size and Mother Ginger twirl and gesticulate. A band of mice (six-feet tall) march back and forth across the lawn. Pride of place goes to a 15-foot tall Christmas tree decorated with 3,500 lights. The house is covered with so many bulbs that he's lost count.

Of course you want to know the *why* of all this and there's a good reason. "I started it some years ago after my last chemotherapy. I went into remission and decided to do this for the children every year. Now the kids expect it and I have discovered I am a bit of a ham."

Things get going around December 10th when Mr. Polizzotto begins his emcee duties and a crew of a half dozen people, dressed in character costumes (Mickey Mouse, Barney, and Rudolf the Red-Nosed Reindeer), mingle with the nightly crowds in this electrified corner of Bensonhurst. Mr. Polizzotto chooses his holiday favorites from Bing Crosby, Frank Sinatra, Nat King Cole, and Tchaikovsky to underscore the scene. Many visitors donate money, which he sends to cancer-related charities. Lights and action begin about 6 P.M. and last until 1 A.M. They turn the music off at 10 P.M. The live characters are not there after December 25th, but the display stays until January 6th.

You may find other houses in this and other neighborhoods with mechanized figures and illumination, but if you want to find the spirit of Christmas, it's right here.

Ice Skating and Hot Chocolate

Some places to go when you want your holiday on ice and then a hot chocolate warmup. You can rent skates at all of the rinks. To buy skates, the specialist is **Peck and Goodie,** 919 Eighth Ave. [54th/55th] 246-6123.

DOWNTOWN

SKATE: **4 World Trade Center,** outdoors on the second level. 524-4386.

HOT CHOCOLATE: **Yaffa's Tea Room,** 19 Harrison St. [Greenwich] 966-0577.

CHELSEA

SKATE: **Sky Rink at Chelsea Piers** [23rd and the Hudson] 336-6100. Two indoor rinks, one for general skating and one for hockey. The aspiring skaters here give a show each December. Routines are performed by children as young as six who are learning and practicing there. The oldest performers are teenagers.

HOT CHOCOLATE: **Le Gamin,** 183 Ninth Ave. [21st] 243-8864.

MIDTOWN

SKATE: **Rivergate Ice Rink,** 401 E. 34th St. [1st Ave.]
689-0035. A small outdoor rink.
HOT CHOCOLATE: **Chez Laurence Patisserie,**
245 Madison Ave. [38th] 683-0284.

SKATE: **Rockefeller Center** 332-7654. For many people,
this is the classic image of skating in New York City, in the
canyon of Rockefeller Center.
HOT CHOCOLATE: **Café S. F. A.,** in Saks, 611 Fifth
Ave. [49th/50th] 940-4080.

CENTRAL PARK

SKATE: **Wollman Rink,** mid-Park at 62nd St. 396-1010.
HOT CHOCOLATE: **La Maison du Chocolat,** 25 E. 73rd
St. [5th/Madison] 744-7117.

UPPER EAST SIDE

SKATE: **Ice Studio,** 1034 Lexington Ave. [73rd/74th] 2nd
floor 535-0304. This is a charming indoor rink that does a lot
of teaching. It's rather small as ice rinks go, with a mirror
along one side and a ballet barre on the other. The skaters
are not racing around in circles, but are gliding through
their routines. "It's like a dance studio on ice," says Bill
Aquilino who has been an ice dancing teacher for 10 years.
HOT CHOCOLATE: **Serendipity 3,** 225 E. 60th St. [2nd/
3rd] 838-3531.

SKATE: **Lasker Rink,** 110th St. and Lenox 396-1010.
HOT CHOCOLATE: **Ciao Bella,** 27 E. 92nd St. [Mad-
ison] 831-5555.

January 6th

*J*ANUARY 6TH is the traditional end of the holiday season. It is variously called Little Christmas, Twelfth Night, Three Kings' Day, and Epiphany. The religious significance of the day is that the Baby Jesus was presented to the three wise men (Christmas used to be celebrated on this day until the eighteenth century change in the calendar that reduced the number of days in the year by 12). The secular tradition of Twelfth Night, celebrated on the previous evening, was a time for parties, games, and other festivities.

El Dio de Tres Reyes, or Three Kings' Day, on January 6th is celebrated with a parade sponsored by ***El Museo del Barrio,*** 1230 Fifth Ave. [104th] 831-7272. Tradition has it that the kings, Melchior, Gaspar, and Balthazar, carried the gifts of gold, frankincense, and myrrh to the Child. Preparations for the child-centered event begin in October when El Museo invites hundreds of schoolchildren in to make drawings and paintings of the story of the kings. The night of January 5th, children place hay and water in a shoe box so that the kings' camels or horses can refresh themselves. All of these children, as many as 2,000, march in the parade with their creations. They are accompanied by musicians, including the popular singer and quattro (a four stringed guitar) player, Yomo Toro, and a set of 30 foot high papier-mâché kings. Local artists, dressed as the kings, distribute favors and small gifts to children along the route and spend the post-parade hours visiting children in hospitals. The parade begins at 10 A.M. in front of El Museo, goes east on 104th St. to 3rd Ave., up to 116th St., over to Lexington Ave., then down to 106th St., and back to the museum.

It is traditional for Greeks to dive for a cross on January 6th. The morning service at **St. Nicholas Church,** 155 Cedar St. [West/Washington] 227-0773, includes a trip to the waterside. The waters are blessed and a wooden cross is thrown into the harbor near Battery Park. Men and teenage boys dive into the water. The one who retrieves the cross is guaranteed good fortune for the year.

Kids' Activities - Part 1

*A*MAHL: ***The Little Orchestra Society,*** 704-2100, performs Gian Carlo Menotti's opera, *Amahl and the Night Visitors* in Avery Fisher Hall at Lincoln Center. Mr. Menotti created this staging (which uses some live animals) for the Society in 1981. Tickets required.

BLESSING OF THE ANIMALS: On Christmas Eve, children and adults bring their pets to ***Central Presbyterian Church,*** 593 Park Ave. [64th] 838-0808, for the blessing of the animals. Dogs, cats, parrots, (and, on one occasion, some worms) attend either the 2:30 or 4:30 P.M. church service. The collection taken is distributed to several animal charities.

BROADWAY KIDS: Broadway Kids is a revue combining carols and show tunes for kids and performed by kids who are in the casts of various Broadway shows and some daytime soaps. It takes place at the ***Tribeca Performing Arts Center,*** 199 Chambers St. [Greenwich/West] 346-8510, in early December. Tickets required.

BRYANT PARK: *Country Living* magazine sponsors a Holiday in Bryant Park with 75,000 lights, artisan created life-size animals, and an activity tent. Bring the kids for cookie, puppet, and ornament making. Things get going around Thanksgiving and run through January 6th. Free. 649-3201.

CIRCUS: The little big top over the one ring of the **Big Apple Circus** goes up in Damrosch Park at Lincoln Center in the holiday season. A brand–new show is created each year by circus founders Paul Binder and Michael Christensen, using favorite characters like Barry Lubin's Grandma or invited guest artists like Mummenschanz. Live music, elephants, equestrian acts, and clowns add up to a dazzling and exciting package when wrapped by the Big Apple artistry. 268-2500. Tickets required.

MOVIES AND TV: You can spend a happy hour or so wandering in the **American Museum of the Moving Image,** 35th St. at 36th St. Astoria 718-784-0077. The kids can work on their animation techniques using the many interactive exhibits. When fatigue sets in you can see a movie. Shorts and serials are screened in the Red Grooms-decorated Tut's Fever Movie Palace each afternoon. During the holidays there are full-length weekday matinees. Screenings are free with museum admission. . .**The Museum of Television and Radio,** 25 W. 52nd St. [5th/6th] 621-6600, makes a point of scheduling holiday screenings. Look for *Charlie Brown's Christmas* or holiday episodes of *Fraggle Rock*. All screenings are free with museum admission.

*P*AGEANTS: A Pageant of the Holy Nativity is performed at **St. Bartholomew's,** Park Ave. and 50th St. 378-0227. The professional choir at St. Bart's provides backup for this family event.

Christmas Uptown is what the **Cathedral of St. John the Divine,** 1047 Amsterdam Ave. [112th] 662-2133, calls their family program. Jugglers and Morris dancers, Messiah excerpts, and a carol sing-along. Tickets required.

PARTIES: In early December look for the **Museum of the City of New York's** Share the Season party celebrating Christmas, Hanukkah, Kwanzaa and Three Kings' Day. Craft activities and entertainment for children and their parents. Museum admission plus donation of a new toy or canned food. . .The Children's Holiday Party started in 1970. It is a fundraiser for the museum's family and children's programming. Activities, entertainment, and snacks. 5th Ave. and 103rd St. 534-1672. Tickets required.

The lovely 1765 **Morris-Jumel Mansion,** 65 Jumel Terrace [160th] 923-8008, holds a family holiday party each

December. The house is decorated in Colonial style, with lots of greens and holly. "There is no Christmas tree – that was a Victorian custom," says director Peter Apgar, "but there is food, caroling, and children's activities. All of it is meant to evoke the scaled-down holiday celebrated in Colonial America." Events free with museum admission.

PUPPETS: Ralph Lee, New York City's Master Puppeteer, sets up shop in the Main Building at the New York Botanical Gardens, 200th St. and Southern Blvd. Bronx 718-817-8700. *The Puppet Theatre* gives two or three performances each day beginning mid-December until the first week of January. Mr. Lee designs these shows for bread-box-size, hand-held puppets. You see both the actor and puppet but the focus is on the puppet. There is a small additional charge beyond garden admission. . .Another puppet theatre is located in Macy's.

READINGS: Each year the *Pierpont Morgan Library,* 29 E. 36th St. [Madison] 685-0610, exhibits the original manuscript of Charles Dickens' *A Christmas Carol.* As a special treat, on the first Sunday in December, the library holds a Family Day that includes a reading of the famous story. Tickets required for the reading.

At the *Old Merchant's House,* 29 E. 4th St. [Lafayette/Bowery] 777-1089, director Mimi Sherman reads "A Visit from St. Nicholas" each year to children ages 3 to 7. The nineteenth century house is decorated for the holidays and light refreshments are served. They also hold a reading of *A Christmas Carol.*

THEATRE: Charles Dickens' *A Christmas Carol* is presented as a musical spectacular in **Madison Square Garden's theatre** from late November to early January. Seventh Ave. [31st/33rd]. Tickets required. 465-6741.

Between Thanksgiving and Christmas, the **Interborough Repertory Theater** gives its performances in theatres around the tristate area. Between Christmas and New Year's they settle into a Manhattan venue for their one-hour Broadway musicals specially devised for children from ages 5 to 11. Shows in their repertory you might see are *The Little Match Girl, A Christmas Carol, The Nutcracker,* or *The Gift of the Magi.* Modest ticket prices. 206-6875.

TOYS: A visit to *The Forbes Magazine Galleries,* 62 Fifth Ave. [11th/12th] 206-5548, can be magical. The collections of model airplanes, boats, and soldiers are intriguingly displayed in small rooms. The Land of Counterpane, an exhibit based on Robert Louis Stevenson's poem of the same name, puts the child into the perspective of the child in the poem. Free.

There's always a good reason to stop by the ***Museum of the City of New York,*** Fifth Ave and 103rd St. 534-1672. At the holidays, with a child in tow, be sure to head to the toy collection. The teddy bears, toy theatres, puzzles, and games, some well-worn and some pristine, are an evocative display of childhoods past for adults and bits of history for the hand-held game generation. The dollhouse collection includes the one made by artist Florine Stettheimer. Its picture gallery holds miniatures of paintings by Marcel Duchamp and others.

F.A.O. Schwarz, 767 Fifth Ave. [58th] 644-9400, is a toy emporium, playground, and wonderland for the thousands who line up every year just to get inside during the holiday season. There is the Star Wars shop designed by Lucas Films, a doll collection that contains many fair creatures exclusive to F.A.O. Schwarz, and a Barbie boutique where she appears, in one manifestation, as George Washington. The F.A.O. Schweetz department dispenses 22 different colors of M&M's and countless jelly beans.

WORKSHOPS: The Children's Museum of Manhattan, 212 W. 83rd St. [Broadway/Amsterdam] 721-1234, which is always full of activities and workshops for kids, is even more so in December. CMOM celebrates Hanukkah, Christmas, and Kwanzaa with art and music programs that teach the meaning of each celebration. Free with museum admission.

Kwanzaa

*T*HE WORD *KWANZAA* comes from a longer Swahili expression meaning "the first fruits of the harvest."

The holiday Kwanzaa was started in 1966 by Dr. Maulana Karenga as a way to bring African Americans close to their cultural heritage through a week of family-centered activities. Seven principles of personal and community conduct are food for thought in the days from December 26th-January 1st. A child lights the kinara, a seven-branched candle holder with one black, three red and three green candles, while the family gathers to discuss one of the principles each day. These are: Umoja (Unity), Kujichagulia (Self-Determination), Ujima (Collective Responsibility and Work), Ujamaa (Cooperative Economics), Nia (Purpose), Kuumba (Creativity) and Imani (Faith). Ancestors are honored and a libation is poured and drunk. Friends come together in private homes to share meals. Increasingly, there are public Kwanzaa celebrations.

The Museum for African Art, 593 Broadway [Houston/ Prince] 966-1313, offers programming several times during the Kwanzaa week. They focus on one of the seven themes, tell stories and give the children a gallery visit. There is a small extra charge on top of museum admission.

One day during the week of Kwanzaa, the **American Museum of Natural History,** Central Park West at 79th St. 769-5100, turns the Hall of Ocean Life into an African Marketplace. Dancers, drummers, and griots (storytellers) perform all afternoon on the dance floor under the Great Blue Whale while artisans sell craft wares on the balcony in front of the porpoises and penguins. Events are free with museum admission.

The Jacob Javits Convention Center, 655 W. 34th St. [12th] 216-2000, is the site of Kwanzaa Expo, 718-379-9291, in early December. Jose Ferrer started the Expo in 1982 as a place where people could learn about the holiday and purchase kinaras, candles, and other craft items. It quickly outgrew several venues in town before it settled at the Javits, where over 300 vendors sell art, clothing, greeting cards, and foods. There are workshops and entertainment, some geared to children and teen-agers. Admission charged.

The Studio Museum in Harlem, 144 W. 125th St. [Lenox/Adam Clayton Powell, Jr.] 864-4500, has a family program on an aspect of the holiday each December.

To learn more: Two books by Dr. Karenga are *Kwanzaa Origin, Concepts and Practice* and *The African-American Holiday of Kwanzaa: A Celebration of Family, Community & Culture*. *A Kwanzaa Keepsake* by Jessica B. Harris serves as a cookbook, a personal memoir, and a scrapbook for you.

Messiahs

*I*N 1770, HANDEL'S MESSIAH had its American premiere at the original Trinity Church. **Trinity Church,** 74 Trinity Place [Rector/Thomas], has performed it countless times ever since. The Trinity Choir and orchestra give two full performances each Christmas season. Call the music office, 602-0873. Tickets required. Here are some of the other annual Messiahs.

PERFORMANCES

Cathedral of St. John the Divine, 1047 Amsterdam Ave. [112th] 662-2133. Several choirs, soloists, and an orchestra in the specially lit cathedral. Tickets required.

Grace Church, 802 Broadway [10th] 254-2000 ext. 105. The Grace Church Choral Society and Chamber Orchestra gives a performance around mid-December. Tickets required.

The **Oratorio Society** likes to say that Andrew Carnegie built the hall for them. Mr. Carnegie was president of the group and his wife sang with them when conductor Walter Damrosch convinced him to build Carnegie Hall. Whether it's true or not, it is certain that the Oratorio Society has sung Handel's Messiah every year since 1875 in Carnegie Hall, 57th St. and Seventh Ave. You can get tickets to hear the 170 singers by calling 247-4199.

St. Joseph's, 371 Ave. of the Americas [Waverly/Washington] 741-1274, is the oldest Catholic church structure in Manhattan. There's a yearly Messiah performance on a Sunday afternoon with organ and choir, followed by a carol sing-along.

St. Thomas Church, Fifth Ave. and 53rd St. 757-7013, ext. 3027. The St. Thomas Choir of men and boys and the Concert Royal Orchestra give two performances.

The National Chorale has been giving their full concert performances of the Messiah since 1967. They also produce an annual Messiah Sing-In, where they provide the soloists and you are the chorus. Avery Fisher Hall, Lincoln Center, 721-6500.

SING-ALONGS

At the **Riverside Church,** 490 Riverside Dr. [120th/122th] 870-6700, the audience joins the Riverside choir and soloists. If you don't have your own score, you can purchase one. Suggested donation.

St. Bartholomew's Church, Park Ave. and 50th St. 378-0227, has professionals on the altar to sing the solos and keep everyone on track. If you don't have your own score, the church will lend you one.

The West Village Chorale holds a Messiah sing-along in **St. Luke-in-the-Fields,** 487 Hudson St. [Grove/Barrow] 570-7301. They pass out the sheet music, give you some guidance, then off you go.

An operatic guest star and the Downtown Symphony Orchestra back you up at the **Tribeca Performing Arts Center Messiah Sing-In,** 199 Chambers St. [Greenwich/West] 346-8510. Early December. Free.

Music Around Town

The Boys Choir of Harlem, and as of 1997, *The Girls Choir of Harlem,* give yearly performances in Lincoln Center and Carnegie Hall. 289-1815.

Carnegie Hall, 881 Seventh Ave. [57th] 247-7800, is where you go to hear annual holiday concerts by The Vienna Choir Boys, The New York Pops with Skitch Henderson, and The New York String Orchestra. The Colors of Christmas is an all-star celebration with pop and R&B performers.

The Chamber Music Society of Lincoln Center gives three performances of Bach's Brandenburg Concertos during the holiday season in Alice Tully Hall. 875-5788.

The Dessoff Choirs were founded in 1924. Each year they perform a part sacred, part secular concert that ends with a carol sing-along. Tickets required. 935-2551.

In Puerto Rico, strolling carolers, called *parranderos,* go from house to house. After singing and taking some refreshment, the members of each household join the singers on their walk though the town. In New York City, *El Museo del Barrio,* 1230 Fifth Ave. [104th] 831-7272, kicks off their holiday season the week before Thanksgiving with *parrandas* performed by Sonido Costeño, singing and playing traditional instruments in the museum halls.

The Metropolitan Museum of Art, Fifth Ave. and 82nd St., holds their Christmas concerts near the tree in the Medieval Sculpture Hall. Regulars are the two a cappella choirs Chanticleer and Pomerium, the Aulos Ensemble for baroque music, Anonymous 4 for medieval singing, and Quartetto Gelato, a funky classical group (tenor, oboe, accordion, and cello) who slip in some gypsy music and tangos. 570-3949.

The 180-member *New York City Gay Men's Chorus* gives their holiday concert each year in Carnegie Hall. 247-7800.

The New York Philharmonic Orchestra presents several concerts each holiday season with different guest artists each year. Tickets required. 721-6500.

The 85 singers who make up the *Riverside Choral Society* perform a major sacred work each year. 780-2181.

While there is a tree at the South St. Seaport, the best reason to wander down to Front St. is to see and hear the *Chorus Tree.* Visiting school choirs and the St. Cecilia's choir climb onto a tree-shaped stand, where they sing mostly Christmas and some Hanukkah songs. The two daily performances begin the Friday after Thanksgiving and continue until New Year's Day. Free. 732-7678.

The Stonewall Chorale is the oldest continuously performing gay and lesbian chorus in the country. Their annual holiday concert is always a combination of secular and religious music that ends with a carol sing-along. 971-5813.

Z-100's Jingle Ball at Madison Square Garden in the first half of December features more than half a dozen major acts performing over a five hour period. Profits go to local charities. Listen to Z100, 100.3 FM, for details.

Music in Churches

$\mathcal{T}$HERE ARE MESSIAHS ALL OVER TOWN (see the "Messiahs" entry) but if you're looking for alternatives, consider the following:

Cathedral of St. John the Divine, 1047 Amsterdam Ave. [112th]. Christmas carols are sung by the Cathedral Choristers. Dorothy Papadokos accompanies them on the organ. Tickets required. 662-2133.

The Christmas Pageant at the Church of the Heavenly Rest, 2 E. 90th St. [5th] 289-3400, is performed by 100 or so children and some live animals. Traditional carols are sung by a choir.

Gospel Express is a monthly program at ***Canaan Baptist Church,*** 132 W. 116th St. [Lenox/Adam Clayton Powell, Jr.] 866-0301, but the Thanksgiving and Christmas programs are special. There is an all-you-can-eat buffet followed by the performance. Director C. Eugene Cooper brings in gospel ensembles and soloists from near and far. Tickets required.

Stop by ***Grace Church,*** 802 Broadway [10th] 254-2000 ext. 105, on Christmas Eve for their Festival of Lessons and

Carols featuring the Choir of Men and Boys and the St. Cecilia's Choir. Donation.

Christmas Eve at **Riverside Church,** 490 Riverside Dr. [120th/122nd] 870-6700, begins with a carillon concert followed by the choir and bell choir performing a Service of Christmas Lessons and Carols.

In mid–December, **St. Bartholomew's Church,** Park Ave. and 50th St. 378-0227, holds a Joyous Holiday Concert that features the American Boy Choir (James Litton, conductor) with the St. Bartholomew's choir. Organist William Trafka plays the largest pipe organ in the city.

The holiday concert at **St. Ignatius Loyola Church,** 980 Park Ave. [84th] 288-2520, uses the talents of two choirs, several soloists, a harpist and some string players. The star of the show, though, might be considered to be their organ, built by N. P. Mander and installed in 1993. It's the largest mechanical action organ in New York City. Tickets required.

St. Michael's Church, Amsterdam Ave. and 99th St. 678-5432, presents unaccompanied medieval music by the four women who make up the group Anonymous 4. The Festival of Lessons and Carols is sung by a professional choir and is sponsored by a dozen West Side churches. The concert is free, but an offering is collected for a charity. 222-2700.

St Patrick's Cathedral, Fifth Ave. [50th/51st] 753-2261. St. Patrick's Chapel Choir, composed of 20 singers, performs a cappella in an Advent concert in mid–December. Tickets are available at the Parish House, 14 E. 51st St. [Madison].

New Year's Day

Jan. 1

The Poetry Marathon starts at 2 P.M. on New Year's Day and by the time the 150 poets, musicians and playwrights and actors are finished it's 2 A.M. Call The Poetry Project at St. Marks-in-the-Bowery, 131 E. 10th St. [2nd/3rd] 674-0910. Admission charge at the door.

While most museums are closed on New Year's Day, the *Old Merchant's House,* 29 E. 4th St. [Lafayette/Broadway] 777-1089, is dressed up in nineteenth-century holiday style and open for an afternoon reception.

Watch multiple football games and bet on the ponies at the same time. Head out to *Aqueduct Racetrack,* Rockaway Blvd. and 110th St. Queens 718-641-4700, for the traditional opening of the winter season. Take a seat in either the Man o' War Room or the Saratoga Room, where the televisions don't show *Ready, Set, Cook!*

The New York tradition of a movie and a Chinese meal can be supplemented by a visit to the following places, which are open on New Year's Day:

Aquarium for Wildlife Conservation, West 8th and Surf Ave. 718-265-3474

Bronx Zoo/Wildlife Conservation Park, Bronx River Pkwy. and Fordham Rd. 718-367-1010

Ellis Island and Statue of Liberty, 363-3200

Solomon R. Guggenheim Museum, 1071 Fifth Ave. [88th/89th] 423-3500

Museum of Modern Art, 11 W. 53rd St. [5th/6th] 708-9400

National Museum of the American Indian, U.S. Custom House, 1 Bowling Green [State/Whitehall] 668-6624

New York Botanical Garden, 200th St. and Southern Ave. Bronx 718-817-8700

Clubs that don't take the night off:
Eighty-Eight's, 228 W. 10th St. [Bleecker/Hudson] 924-0088, for cabaret entertainment.
Fez, under the Time Cafe, 380 Lafayette St. [Great Jones] 533-7000, has a mix of rock, pop, and folk performers.
Village Vanguard, 178 Seventh Ave. S. [W. 11th] 255-4037. Dr. Michael White brings his New Orleans sextet for the week that includes New Year's Eve. The same great music on New Year's Day.

Every four years, rain or shine, there is a mayor taking the oath of office on *City Hall* steps on January 1st. This happens again in 1998.

New Year's Eve - Part 1

WHETHER YOUR IDEA OF A GREAT NEW YEAR'S EVE is having Champagne and caviar at home or in a restaurant, being with a small group or a half million people, black tie or black jeans, there's no end of options for this night. In addition to all the restaurants and clubs, here are a few ways you can celebrate.

ATHLETIC

Run into the new year with the **New York Road Runners Club,** 9 E. 89th St. [5th/Madison] 860-4455. A 5 kilometer (3.1–mile) fun run is preceded by a costume parade near Tavern on the Green in Central Park. Joggers and walkers are welcome.

CLASSIC

The Waldorf-Astoria opened at 301 Park Ave. [50th] 355-3000, in 1931 and they have been celebrating New Year's Eve there in one form or another ever since. The Waldorf became associated with New Year's when Guy Lombardo and his orchestra began leading the party in the Grand Ballroom. The Waldorf still holds a big black tie bash on the 31st. Dinner, Champagne, dancing to Peter Duchin's orchestra, and entertainment by a headline act will set you back nearly $400.

CLASSICAL

A festive atmosphere suffuses **Bargemusic,** Fulton Ferry Landing, Brooklyn 718-624-4061, where they perform all six Brandenburg Concertos on New Year's Eve. Musicians at Bargemusic perform in front of the skyline of Manhattan. Inside the barge there are catered hors d'oeuvres, desserts, and Champagne during the frequent intermissions. Cellist Fred Sherry calls the Brandenburgs "very concentrated pieces. The breaks make it easier on the musicians and the audience." The musicians ring in the New Year and you can watch the fireworks that are sent aloft at the South Street Seaport. The concert is broadcast nationally on National Public Radio. Tickets required.

Avery Fisher Hall at Lincoln Center is done up in ribbons and flowers for the evening's annual **New York Philharmonic Gala.** Streamers float from the ceiling to the balconies, the orchestra members wear festive attire, and an internationally known soloist takes the spotlight. 721-6500.

DANCE

The Alvin Ailey Dance Company is in town for the month of December. Their New Year's Eve performance always takes note of the holiday, sometimes spelling out the New Year in candles on stage or passing out fans to the audience during *Revelations.* City Center, 131 W. 55th St. [6th/7th] 581-1212.

FIREWORKS

The South Street Seaport brings the New Year in with a fireworks display starting at midnight. Free. 732-7678. . . . Near **Tavern on the Green in Central Park,** there's a round of fireworks at midnight. Free.

New Year's Eve - Part 2

FIRST NIGHT

*F*IRST NIGHT IS A SERIES OF EVENTS, activities, and performances that begin on New Year's Eve morning and continue through midnight. A petting zoo is set up in Bryant Park, and there are stories and performances for children. You can take dance lessons in the afternoon, then strut your stuff under the starlit canopy in Grand Central Station in the evening. Go to a comedy performance at the Public Library, then hop on the free shuttle bus to hear a jazz set at St. Peter's Church. Maybe you'd prefer a trip to the top of the Empire State Building and a midnight skate on the Wollman Rink. All for $20/person, $5 for children under 12. Events are alcohol-free. The First thing you need is a button, which goes on sale in early December. First Night is sponsored by the Grand Central Partnership. 922-9393.

HISTORICAL

If you are in a nineteenth-century mood, you might want to consider the **New Year's Eve Cotillion at Historic Richmond Town,** 441 Clarke Ave. Staten Island 718-351-1611. A midnight supper is served to the guests, many of whom are in costume. Ticket required.

ON THE WATER

For about $200 a person, you can board the **World Yacht** at 9 P.M., enjoy a five course meal, open bar, and band, see in the New Year, and return about 1 A.M. 630-8100. . .On the **Spirit of New York,** it's about $175 for a sit down dinner, open bar, and dancing. Board at 8 P.M. for a four-hour sail. 480-2949.

PERFORMANCES

The **New Year's Eve Concert for Peace at the Cathedral of St. John the Divine,** 1047 Amsterdam [112th], starts during the evening hours. Cathedral artists-in-residence Philippe Petit and Paul Winter may perform on the high wire and the soprano saxophone respectively. Most seating is free; tickets for reserved seating, 662-2133.

The New York Gilbert and Sullivan Players present a G&S operetta on New Year's Eve at Symphony Space, 2537 Broadway [95th] 864-5400. There is a Champagne intermission, and a round of "Auld Lang Syne" with the orchestra.

Riverside Church, 490 Riverside Dr. [120th/122nd] 870-6700, rings in the New Year with a carillon recital, followed by an organ recital and a worship service.

Many Broadway shows have regular performances on New Year's Eve.

TIMES SQUARE

Times Square is of course synonymous with New York's New Year's Eve. By late evening there are a half million people sandwiched into the blocks along Broadway and Seventh Ave. north of One Times Square. When the famous countdown begins, the refurbished glittering ball drops while a ton and a half of confetti flies into the air from thirteen different buildings. 354-0003.

The Nutcracker

*T*HIS IS THE STORY of how the United Nations created a prince.

Peter Boal's British grandfather came to New York in the late 1940s to work at the U.N. Mr. Boal's grandparents were active balletgoers and passed their enthusiasm to their daughter, who, in turn, passed it down another generation. Mr. Boal says, "As soon as my sister and I were able to sit still for three hours, the whole family, three generations, would go to the ballet together. I think I saw my first *Nutcracker* at age 5." By age 9, in 1975, he was no longer in his seat but in the wings, about to make his debut with the New York City Ballet as one of the children in the party scene. "I was terrified and panicked. I did not want to let go of my mother's hand. Judith Fugate, who played my stage mother in the production, took my hand from my mother and led me on stage."

By the age of 12, Mr. Boal had gotten over his stage fright and was dancing the role of the Little Prince. "I was comfortable with the role and sitting on the throne for forty minutes and watching Mikhail Baryshnikov, Suzanne Farrell, Peter Martins, and Elizabeth McBride perform was my idea of a good time."

When he got too old to dance the Little Prince, Mr. Boal put in time as the "bed boy", a soldier doll, a Chinese dancer, and a Spanish dancer, and, at 17, he was a Mouse. At 19, all grown up by ballet standards, he began to portray the Big Prince. "It was exciting since, in a way, I had grown up and was still growing up in this ballet." The Big Prince is the only male role for a principal dancer, which Mr. Boal is, so nine dancers alternate the part during the 45 performances. Every year he watches the kids who are performing. "I remember being one of them. Half of them are so professional and are trying to do everything perfectly; the other half are natural 10 year olds."

He describes *The Nutcracker* as a "joyous experience, flying in the sleigh, the magic bed, waking Clara up, and walking in the snow. The theatre is full of children who are 50 yards away from the whole wonderful experience. They are all dressed up, with looks of awe on their faces when they see those little performers." There is also, no doubt, a Little Prince sitting on the throne watching Mr. Boal, thinking that this is certainly his idea of a good time.

George Balanchine's choreography for Tchaikovsky's *The Nutcracker* has been performed by the **New York City Ballet** each year since 1954. New York State Theatre, 721-6500.

Out on the Town

$\mathcal{E}$VEN NEW YORKERS who console themselves with knowing there's so much to do and never doing any of it tend to get out a bit at the holidays. A few possible itineraries.

AN UPPER EAST SIDE EVENING

We'd start our evening at the *Lobster Club,* 240 E. 80th St. [5th/Madison], 249-6500, for some of Anne Rosenzweig's takes on American food, or at Bobby Flay's *Mesa City,* 1059 Third Ave. [62nd/63rd] 207-1919, for his southwestern specialities. Cap off an evening in this part of town with a stop into the *Carlyle,* 35 E. 76th St. [Madison/ Park] 744-1600, to hear Barbara Carroll at Bemelman's Bar or Bobby Short at Café Carlyle.

AN UPPER WEST SIDE EVENING

You can have a pleasant dinner at *Picholine,* 35 W. 64th St. [Broadway/Central Park West] 724-8585—be sure to sample some of their excellent cheeses, ripened in their own cheese cave. Walk across Broadway to an opera at the *Met,* 721-6500. Change the musical vibrations a bit by ducking into *Iridium,* 44 W. 63rd St. [Columbus/Broadway] 582-2121, for a nightcap and some jazz.

A TIMES SQUARE EVENING

If you're visiting, you'll want to stroll around Times Square, and if you live here, unless you're in the area frequently, you'll want to stroll around, too. That's because these days the area seems to undergo a major transformation every month. Sit down to some vodka and caviar at the festive Russian restaurant *Firebird,* 365 W. 46th St. [8th/9th] 586-0244, then adjourn to the latest Broadway hit. Afterward, stream into *Joe Allen's,* 325 W. 46th St. [8th/9th] 581-6464, with the rest of the theatre-goers and theatre community to talk about the show.

A WEST VILLAGE EVENING

Get a taste of the old Village by having dinner at *Piccolo Angolo,* 621 Hudson St. [Jane] 229-9177. It's a delightful, unpretentious, bustling Italian family restaurant with delicious food at reasonable prices. Walk off the carbohydrates in the area around Bank Street and then belt out show tunes with the crowds, mostly gay, at *Eighty Eight's,* 228 W. 10th St. [Bleecker/Hudson] 924-0088.

AN EAST VILLAGE EVENING

Though *Global 33,* 93 Second Ave. [5th/6th] 477-8427, with its neo-airport style, isn't everyone's idea of the East Village, launch an evening with one of their superb cocktails. Wait in line with everyone at *Hasaki,* 219 E. 9th St. [2nd/3rd] 473-3327, for great sushi, and hit the right club on the right night.

A SOHO/TRIBECA EVENING

Start with a stroll along the waterfront in Hudson River Park, with its views of the Statue of Liberty and Ellis Island. Have dinner at *The Independent,* 179 W. Broadway [Leonard/Worth] 219-2010, a hopping Tribeca restaurant. Then listen to what's new in music at the *Knitting Factory,* 74 Leonard St. [Church/Broadway] 219-3055.

Restaurants for Adults

*H*ERE ARE A FEW OF OUR FAVORITES for a holiday celebration. Any one of these should send you out into the night full of cheer.

Bouley, 120 W. Broadway [Duane] 964-2525. The welcome return of top chef David Bouley.

Chanterelle, 2 Harrison St. [Hudson] 966-6960. David and Karen Waltuck run a restaurant that defines the word 'civilized.' Don't waste the experience with just anybody—go to Chanterelle with your nearest and dearest and celebrate the good things in life.

Follonico, 6 W. 24th St. [5th/6th] 691-6359. Alan Tardi and Karen Bussen's restaurant is sophisticated but completely disarming. Mr. Tardi's lovely Italian food and attentive staff make this restaurant a reliable delight.

Gramercy Tavern, 42 E. 20th St. [Broadway/Park Ave. S.] 477-0777. Proprietor Danny Meyer and chef Tom Colicchio have a large, deservedly popular, lively, bustling top restaurant.

Honmura An, 170 Mercer St. [Houston/Prince] 334-5253. The Japanese eat soba (buckwheat) noodles to celebrate the New Year. This restaurant serves delicious food centered on soba, so celebrate the New Year in fine Japanese style.

Jean George, 1 Central Park West [60th] 299-3900. Jean-Georges Vongerichten's exceptional cooking is featured in this haute moderne restaurant.

Le Refuge, 166 E. 82nd St. [Lexington/3rd] 861-4505, is a country French restaurant with both solid, satisfying food and charming service.

Quilty's, 177 Prince St. [Sullivan/Thompson] 254-1260. A wonderful and pretty Soho restaurant that has a large following for chef Katy Sparks' delicious food.

River Café, 1 Water St. Brooklyn 718-522-5200. This restaurant's kitchen has been something of a finishing school for a number of the city's most successful chefs, so it is possible to eat well here. It's the view, though, that guarantees a memorable evening.

Union Pacific, 111 E. 22nd St. [Park/Lexington] 995-8500. When we're asked to name our favorite chef, we always say Rocco DiSpirito. It's not unusual to find a chef working with ingredients from around the world as he does but it is rare to find such original, deliriously wonderful food. Truly, a chef with the Midas touch.

Zoë, 90 Prince St. [Broadway/Mercer] 966-6722. The quintessential Soho restaurant with lively food and atmosphere and a great, all-American wine list.

Restaurants for Kids

SSUMING THAT YOUR KIDS' BEHAVIOR has rated above coal in the stocking, here are a few places you can all go to and have some fun together.

Bubby's, 120 Hudson St. [N. Moore] 219-0666, has the feel of a country diner – if country diners played Sarah Vaughan. In the heart of Tribeca, Bubby's takes care of the locals and their kids, and they'll take care of yours, too.

Brooklyn Diner, 212 W. 57th St. [Broadway/7th] 581-8900. Burgers and especially good hot dogs in a fun Brooklyn-themed restaurant.

Golden Unicorn, 18 E. Broadway [Catherine] 941-0911. This popular Chinese restaurant isn't geared to kids, but they may enjoy the large, crowded room, and everyone should like the food.

Grimaldi's, 19 Old Fulton St. [Front/Water] Brooklyn 718-858-4300. You can go to the Brooklyn Diner (see above) or to the real Brooklyn instead for the best pizza in the five boroughs (a hotly debated topic, and even people who champion other places acknowledge Grimaldi's as being at least one of the best). Have a walk back over the Brooklyn Bridge.

Popover Café, 551 Amsterdam Ave. [86th/87th] 595-8555. What started as a narrow, one room place has turned into one of the Upper West Side's most popular spots. The popovers are surefire, and there are teddy bears strewn about for comfort, should any be needed.

Serendipity 3, 225 E. 60th St. [2nd/3rd] 838-3531. Over 40 years old now, Serendipity shows no signs of aging – it's still the appealing, deluxe soda shoppe that it's always been. The frozen hot chocolate and frozen mochaccino never let you down.

Sylvia's, 328 Lenox Ave. [126th/127th] 996-0660. Harlem's now-legendary restaurant, known and loved by all, is still serving some tasty Southern food.

THEMES: Whatever you might think, kids love the city's theme restaurants. Among the choices:
Dinersaurus, American Museum of Natural History, Central Park West and 79th St. 769-5100.
Hard Rock Café, 221 W. 57th St. [Broadway/7th] 489-6565.
Harley Davidson Café, 1370 Ave. of the Americas [56th] 245-6000.
Motown Café, 104 W. 57th St. [6th/7th] 581-8030.
Official All Star Café, 1540 Broadway [45th] 840-8326.
Television City Restaurant, 74 W. 50th St. [6th] 333-3388.

Rockefeller Center

$\mathcal{A}$T THE HOLIDAYS, the city's hearth is Rockefeller Center. The pull of the season is impossible to resist when you're anywhere near the area. Even the most curmudgeonly among us tend to revel a bit in the architecture, the tree, and the skaters.

THE TREE. When people speak of The Tree, it's always the Rock Center tree they mean. For more, see the entry "Trees – Part One."

THE CHANNEL GARDENS. The sculptor Valerie Clarebout created the 12 herald angels in the promenade from Fifth Avenue to the Rink. They debuted in 1954. In addition to angels, there are six 'Christmas Cadets,' two drummers, two buglers, a flutist, and a cymbalist.

THE LIGHTS. The late, great Broadway lighting designer Abe Feder designed the spectacular lighting for Rockefeller Center. He developed a special bulb that would project 850 feet upward. In all, 342 lights illuminate the buildings with 500,000 watts. The lighting was unveiled on December 3, 1984 before the lighting of the Christmas tree.

SKATING. As crowded as it can get, a twirl on the ice at Rockefeller Center is a memorable pleasure.

THE RADIO CITY CHRISTMAS SPECTACULAR.
For over 60 years, audiences have been enjoying various versions of the Christmas Spectacular with the always fabulous Rockettes. The show started as a short entertainment between movie screenings. Always popular are the Parade of the Wooden Soldiers and the Living Nativity. 247-4777.

THE RAINBOW ROOM. Heading skyward to the Rainbow Room, about a week before Christmas, the Christmas Teddy Bear Tree appears, decked with over 300 teddy bears sporting Rainbow Room uniforms. The band transforms itself into the Rainbow Reindeer Dance band (trumpets, trombone, tuba, and kazoos) and plays holiday music. On Christmas Day, carolers sing and a reindeer with light-up antlers reads "A Visit from St. Nicholas" to children... Rainbow Promenade Bar: Stop in at the Rainbow Promenade Bar for one of cocktail king Dale DeGroff's special holiday cocktails (see entry "Holiday Drinks for Adults")... Rainbow and Stars: This premiere cabaret boasts views over the city and some of the best performers around. 632-5000.

THE TODAY SHOW. Katie, Matt, Al, et al., and the cheering crowds outside their studio, do a great job of showing off Rockefeller Center and making New York look like the great city that it is.

RESTAURANTS. Food options include the Sea Grill, 19 W. 49th St. [5th/6th] 332-7610 and the American Festival Café, 20 W. 50th St. [5th/6th] 332-7620.

For information on Breakfast with Santa, see entry on "Santa Claus." For tour information, see the entry "Walks and Tours."

Saks Fifth Avenue

*S*aks Fifth Avenue, 611 Fifth Ave. [49th/50th] 753-4000, has gotten into the holiday spirit since it first opened its doors in 1924. In the early days, it was part of the Fifth Ave. Association's Christmas window display competition (there was even an awards dinner at the Waldorf). In 1938, Saks had an exhibition of 'little known' live Santas from around the world. *The New York Times* quoted the director of the store at the time, H. L. Redman, as saying, (forlornly, it seems, from the distance of time): "This Christmas, above all others, the hearts of men are still with the hope that peace, goodwill, and amity among all nations may be achieved."

Over time, there have been a number of variations in the window designs. For many years, the second floor windows were framed by star-topped, illuminated trees. The windows themselves have shown singing couples holding sheet music and angels like the ones across the street in the Channel Gardens. Choir boys have also been represented in the second floor windows while music was piped out onto the street. The windows on the first floor showcased luxurious gifts until the early 1970s when the fantasy and mechanized windows came in.

Enter Spaeth Designs. They have been fabricating the Saks windows since 1977. David Spaeth, the firm's president, says he knew that the first windows they did for Saks, based on the book *Little Women*, were a success because "Saks had to clean the finger marks off of them every day." These were the first holiday windows that did not display merchandise. Since then, the Saks windows have featured children's stories such as *The Velveteen Rabbit,* C.S. Lewis's *The Lion, The Witch, and the Wardrobe,* Broadway shows, Currier and Ives, Hansel and Gretel, and a salute to Carnegie Hall.

A creative team at Saks begins designing the windows in January. Over the course of a year, designers, model makers, animators, costumers, makeup artists, and many others —about 50 people in all—work on a display. The figures in the Saks windows are somewhere between two-thirds and three-quarters life size, which means they require more detail than a smaller figure. "If you put a button on a costume, you have to put the buttonhole there, too." The six holiday windows are unveiled the Tuesday before Thanksgiving at 6 P.M. There is music and hot chocolate.

The newest Saks holiday tradition is the silent auction of the tree stationed on the main floor atrium near the escalators. What entices people to bid and others to simply come look are the ornaments by Christopher Radko. Mr. Radko is the best known of contemporary ornament makers, and his ornaments are very collectible. Mr. Radko contributes his ornaments to the tree, Saks contributes the space, and every penny goes to a charity selected for that year. The auction takes place before Christmas. Call for details.

Santa Claus

*I*N THE OLD DAYS, it was more than getting your ho–ho–hos down.

Charles W. Howard, the Macy's Santa for three decades beginning in the mid-1930s, opened the Charles W. Howard Santa Claus School in 1937 in Albion, N.Y. The school trained Santas for department stores, teaching its students makeup, child psychology, and other relevant subjects. Graduates received a B.S.C. degree.

The tradition of Santa Claus, brought with the Dutch settlers to Manhattan, developed with two New York writers, Washington Irving and Clement Clarke Moore. Mr. Irving published his humorously skewed *Knickerbocker's History of New York* in 1809, in which Irving invents or embellishes many of the trappings and traits that we now associate with Santa. Moore's immensely popular poem, "A Visit from St. Nicholas," published in 1823, created a public relations bonanza for the jolly old elf.

The Santa Claus school has moved to Michigan, and there are no longer any Santa Clauses in New York, to our knowledge, with a B.S.C. Nevertheless, there are some good ones that should make kids smile.

After the **Macy's Santa** comes to town in the Thanksgiving Day Parade, he takes up residence on the eighth floor of the store at W. 34th St. and Herald Square. Children can visit him there, tell him their wishes, and have a photo taken.

Have breakfast with Santa and take an ice skating lesson at Rockefeller Center. On weekends starting in late November, then daily the week before Christmas, a hearty winter breakfast is served up at the **American Festival Café,** 20 W. 50th St. [5th/6th]. Santa skates with the kids and hands out a souvenir of the event. Seatings start at 7:30 A.M. 246-6699, reservations.

Father Christmas strolls the streets and piers of **South Street Seaport** during the day handing out candy canes. Usually dressed in a flannel shirt and red pants, he puts on his formal red jacket only when he performs with the Chorus Tree. Look for him from the day after Thanksgiving until Christmas Eve. Bring your camera as there is no official photographer at the Seaport. 732-7678.

At the **Church of the Intercession,** 555 W. 155th St. [Broadway] 283-6200, St. Nicholas leads everyone in a procession to Clement Clarke Moore's grave two blocks away in Trinity Cemetery. See more in the entry "Clement Clarke Moore."

Lord & Taylor, 424 Fifth Ave. [39th] 391-3344, has a Santa on the seventh floor in the children's department. Call for their schedule.

Santa Lucia Day

$\mathcal{T}$HE ORIGINS OF SANTA LUCIA DAY, a Swedish tradition celebrated on December 13th, are fuzzy but it is likely some combination of martyrdom, the solstice, and a newspaper contest.

There are stories about a young Sicilian girl named Lucia who was martyred on December 13th, 304 A.D., though exactly what this has to do with Sweden's day of light is anybody's guess. The part of the celebration with candles has to do with Swedish traditions on the darkest day of the year, which isn't December 13th, but never mind. A Swedish newspaper held a contest for a Lucia in 1927, dubiously implying a connection to ancient Nordic traditions, that captured the imagination. In any case, if you think of a blond Swedish girl, dressed in white, with candles on her head, singing the Italian song "Santa Lucia," and serving saffron buns and coffee for breakfast, you'll have the idea.

The Swedish Seamen's Church, 5 E. 48th St. [5th/Madison] 832-8443, sponsors two performances of Santa Lucia singers each year, one in the afternoon and one in the evening. The Seamen's Church is small so they schedule performances at other venues. Tickets required.

At the restaurant **Christer's,** 145 W. 55th St. [6th/7th] 974-7224, Lucia singers informally pass through the dining rooms at lunch and dinner. Chef Christer Larsson serves up plates of the traditional foods: mustard-glazed ham, herrings, beet salad, and Jansson's Temptation, a potato and anchovy casserole. "For the hard core," he says, "we serve lutefisk," a cod that has been preserved with lye.

Singers come in the evening to **Aquavit,** 13 W. 54th St. [5th/6th] 307-7311, where a Swedish Christmas menu is served during most of December. Owner Hakan Swahn says, "It's what you would find on the traditional Swedish Christmas buffet but is served in three courses in New York."

The American Scandinavian Foundation holds a bazaar each year full of products from the north countries. Sweaters, linens, greeting cards, books, and plenty of foods – herrings, jams, teas, and chocolate. Santa Lucia singers are on hand one night. Call for dates and location. 879-9779.

The American Scandinavian Society, 245 E. 49th St. [2nd/3rd] 751-0714, holds a black tie Christmas Ball on the first Friday of December in the Metropolitan Club which includes a Lucia procession.

Shopping - Gifts

WHEN THE NUMBER OF DAYS LEFT UNTIL CHRIST-MAS goes into single digits and we still don't have gifts for the people hardest to shop for on our gift list, we pull out *this* list.

Adresse, 226 Elizabeth St. [Houston/Spring] 226-7462. This is the American outpost of the Parisian specialty shop Marie Papier. Notebooks, notecards, boxes, and other pre-electronic desktop accessories. . .***Ad Hoc,*** 410 W. Broadway [Spring] 925-2652. Their selection of soaps and bath products from around the world always brings us back, but they have other bath, kitchen, and houseware items that make good gifts. . . ***Alberene Scottish Cashmere,*** 435 Fifth Ave. [38th/39th] 3rd Floor, 689-0151. The best source of cashmere in NYC. Alberene carries every style of cashmere sweater, cape, throw, and accessory in over 100 colors at wholesale prices. . .***Books of Wonder,*** 16 W. 18th St. [5th/6th] 989-3270. When you are looking for Babar and Curious George and the best in contemporary children's books, go here. . .***Chelsea Antiques Building,*** 110 W. 25th St. [6th/7th] 929-0909. Start at the top on the twelfth floor and work your way down. In the building is a café, a cash machine, and shops with plenty of variety in all price ranges. . .*Felissimo,* 10 W. 56th St. [5th/6th] 247-5656. As zen as shopping over the holidays can get: a pretty store where the home furnishings are selected with a discerning eye. . .*Game Show,* 474 Sixth Ave. [11th/12th] 633-6328, 1240 Lexington Ave. [83rd] 472-8011. Not only do they have the classic board games, they always have the best of the new games. Ask them to recommend something and you'll walk away with something good. . .For gift baskets: *Manhattan Fruitier,* 686-0404, and *Chelsea Gift Baskets* in Chelsea Market, 75 Ninth Ave. [15th/16th] 727-1111. . .*La Maison de la Fausse Fourrure,* 1045 Madison Ave. [79th/80th] 639-9197. So far, fake fur hasn't gotten anyone's dander up. The fake fur coats, slippers, handbags, scarves and other items are as stylish as you could want. . .*Marion Design for Dining,* 401 E. 58th St. [1st/Sutton] 888-0894. Marion Johnson's well-chosen vintage, contemporary, and custom tabletop items range from glassware to serving pieces, dishes, place cards, even knife rests. . .*Moss,* 146 Greene St. [Houston/Prince] 226-2190. Murray Moss has a keen sense of design and scopes out the best from around the world. You'll find things, mostly housewares, that are beautiful and practical, beautiful and less practical, and sometimes funny. . .*Mxyplyzyk,* 123 and 125 Greenwich Ave. [13th] 989-4300, popular since the day it opened, has gifts for the home, always chosen with care. . . *Ooo Baby,* 153 Ludlow St. [Stanton/Rivington] 673-5524. Liz Prince's charming clothes for kids (mostly girls) include Polar Fleece jumpers, a Red Riding Hood Polar Fleece cape, and hand-knit sweaters. . .*Time Will Tell,* 962 Madison Ave. [75th/76th] 861-2663, sells everything from simple watches to the ultra-expensive, both new and vintage.

Shopping - Good Deals

*T*HERE ARE CERTAIN RITES OF PASSAGE before you can call yourself a New Yorker. One of these is developing the instinct to avoid paying retail.

We asked Sara Dworken, publisher of *Good Buy USA*, a comprehensive bi-weekly publication devoted to sample sales and other bargains, to help people hone that instinct. Her advice follows.

You can wait to do your holiday shopping until the after-Christmas sales or you can go to that unique New York experience, the sample sale. Savings typically range from 50 to 80 percent off retail. The holiday season is an especially good time to pick up great deals.

Some things you should know before attending a sample sale: Call to verify dates, times, and location. Try to get there the first day of the sale for the best selection. Ask about stock and size availability, if try-ons are allowed, and methods of payment. There are no returns. They're generally closed on weekends.

The following is a partial list of designers, sample sale houses (which frequently represent more than one designer), and showrooms open by appointment, that have sales throughout the holiday season. Call for details.

SHOWROOMS OPEN BY APPOINTMENT

Giesswein, 499 Seventh Ave. [37th/38th] 14th floor 629-3260. Giesswein carries their own label high-quality Austrian boiled wool jackets for men and women.

Jamak, 200 W. 70th St. [Amsterdam] #12C 787-0278. Jamak's showroom carries women's clothing by designers such as Gruppo Americano, Lulu Bravo, and Badgley Mischka. Suits come in all sizes, and they will special order any suit in your size. Prices are wholesale.

Le Firme, 37 W. 57th St. [5th/6th] Suite 401 888-3433. Le Firme carries an array of designer accessories for men and women. They have silk ties, wallets, scarves, and handbags by European designers at wholesale pricesor below.

SAMPLE SALE HOUSES

Showroom Seven, 498 Seventh Ave. [37th/38th] 24th floor 643-4810. Sales feature clothing and accessories by Erickson Beaman, Anna Sui, Lianne Barnes, Ghost, and Whistle.

Soifer Haskins, 718-747-1656. Soifer Haskins represents Donna Karan, Emanuel Ungaro, Escada, Louis Féraud, and Malo cashmere. Most sales are held at Parsons School of Design. Ask to be put on their mailing list.

SSS Samples Inc., 134 W. 37th St. [Broadway/7th] 2nd floor 947-8748, represents Betsey Johnson, Nicole Miller, Accessories, Kenar, Item, Cynthia Rowley, Mark Eisen, and Mevisto.

During November and December, *Good Buy USA* will fax you an individual issue that includes the holiday sales, for a $10 fee. 800-303-2163.

Shopping - Hobbies and Pastimes

*H*ERE ARE SOME STORES when you're looking for a gift for someone with a hobby, special interest, or other obsession.

BROADWAY MUSICALS: Footlights Records, 113 E. 12th St. [3rd/4th] 533-1572. If it was recorded, it's here.

CHESS: The Village Chess Shop, 230 Thompson St. [W.3rd/ Bleecker] 475-9580. Boards, chess pieces, travel sets, time clocks, and books.

COINS: Stack's Rare Coins, 123 W. 57th St. [6th/7th] 582-2580. America's oldest dealer with a large assortment of paper and metal currencies.

COOKBOOKS: Head up to ***Kitchen Arts and Letters,*** 1435 Lexington Ave. [93rd/94th] 876-5550, for a store of new and used cookbooks, with a most helpful staff.

JEWELRY MAKING: Myron Toback, 25 W. 47th St. [5th/ 6th] 398-8300. This 'hardware store to the jewelry industry' sells findings, tools, and chains, in an astounding array.

MAPS: Look at the selection of old maps at ***Argosy Bookstore,*** 116 E. 59th St. [Lexington/Park] 753-4455, on the second floor after you check out the $10 bin at street level.

MOVIE MEMORABILIA: *Jerry Ohlinger's Movie Material Store,* 242 W. 14th St. [7th/8th] 989-0869. Posters, photos, magazines, postcards, and other movie collectibles.

MURDER MYSTERIES: *Partners & Crime,* 44 Greenwich Ave. [6th/7th] 243-0440. They have a good selection and do well at recommending for all tastes.

NEW YORK: The shop at the ***Museum of the City of New York,*** Fifth Ave. and 103rd St. 534-1672, has posters, toys used in street games, and tee shirts with subway prints.

PENS: *The Fountain Pen Hospital,* 10 Warren St. [Church/Broadway] 964-0580, sells new and vintage pens at good prices.

QUILTS: *Laura Fisher,* 1050 Second Ave. [56th] 838-2596, in the Manhattan Art and Antiques Center, is loaded with antique and vintage pieces.

SNOWDOMES: *It's a Mod, Mod World,* 85 First Ave. [5th/6th] 460-8004, for kitschy ones and the ***OK Harris Gallery,*** 383 Broadway [Broome/Grand] 431-3600, for the limited edition art-inspired ones of Don Celender.

TEAM SPORTS: *Gerry Cosby Sporting Goods* at Madison Square Garden, Seventh Ave. and 33rd St. 563-6464. The clothes the pros wear and the equipment they use when they play baseball, basketball, football, and hockey.

WOODWORKING: *Garrett Wade,* 161 Ave. of the Americas [Spring/Vandam] 807-1155. A great resource for anyone who works with wood, and they couldn't be nicer here.

Stress Relievers

*E*VEN IN THOSE YEARS when you've gotten into the swing of the holidays, there can be a certain amount of stress associated with so much merriment. Here are a few ways to keep your spirits up.

PERSONAL SHOPPING SERVICES: The major department stores all have personal shopping services to make things easier.

Bergdorf's Personal Shopping Dept., 872-8757.
Bloomingdale's Shopping Services, 705-2000.
Lord & Taylor Red Rose Personal Shopping, 391-3519.
Macy's Buy Appointment, 494-4181.
Saks One on One Personal Shopping Services, 940-4145.

If you're ready to do some serious shopping damage in a variety of places, you may also want to call *Good Buy USA.* You tell them your particular shopping needs and they'll match you up with a personal shopper who will accompany you to showrooms. 800-303-2163.

MASSAGE: Down the steps into the herbed and spiced air of *Carapan,* 5 W. 16th St. [5th/6th] 633-6220, you enter a spa designed to relieve you of stress, worldly cares, and $75 for a great massage.

FACIALS: For over 50 years, **Georgette Klinger,** 501 Madison Ave. [52nd/53rd] 838-3200, and 978 Madison Ave. [76th] 744-6900, has been making the skin of New Yorkers glow.

We're partial to **Mamie's Skin Care Center,** 29 Washington Square West [MacDougal] 260-9372. Mamie McDonald does exceptional facials, body wraps, and aromatherapy.

SPAS: There is an increasing number of spas in town. A few choices:

Origins Feel-Good Spa, Pier 62 Chelsea Piers [23rd] 336-6780, for massages and facials.

Osaka Health Center, 50 W. 56th St. [5th/6th] 682-1778. Shiatsu, sauna, aromatherapy, Japanese hot and cold tubs.

Peninsula, 700 Fifth Ave. [55th] 247-2200, is the most complete spa in the city.

Susan Ciminelli Day Spa, 601 Madison Ave. [57th/58th] 688-5500, does scrubs, aromatherapy, and reflexology.

MUSIC: A December afternoon at the **Cloisters** with the **Waverly Consort** is an uncommonly peaceful and transporting experience. The group was founded in 1965 by Michael and Kay Jaffee when they were students at NYU (the group is named for Waverly Place). Mr. Jaffee says, "The Cloisters is an ideal place to present medieval music from England, Spain, and France from the tenth to the fifteenth centuries. The instruments are close copies of the originals and include the citole, a medieval mandolin, a rack of handbells that are hit with hammers, and the straight trumpet, which is six feet long, has no valves, and is played only with air pressure." Tickets. 650-2281.

Ten Places To Be When It's Snowing

WHEN IT SNOWS IN NEW YORK, the clock resets to another time. It gets quieter. People walk through **Central Park** as they have done for decades, allowing themselves a bit of wonder. When you see photographs of people enjoying the park in the snow from the last century, it is remarkable how little has changed. A walk around the reservoir, with its views to Midtown, is especially elating. Central Park is perhaps the best place to be during a snowfall, but there are others that have a special appeal.

Anglers and Writers, 420 Hudson St. [St. Luke's] 675-0810. When a nor'easter is blowing through town, warm up at this comfortable Village spot with a pot of tea. If you come without company and without a book, borrow a book from their shelves.

Barnes and Noble on Union Square, 33 E. 17th St. [Broadway/Park Ave. South] on the 4th floor 253-0810. When you want a larger selection of books, head over to this Barnes and Noble, where you can sit by the windows looking out over Union Square and, as you did in your university library, dream and doze.

As it turns to dusk, snow and the lights of the city add an extra bit of magic to your vantage point on the **Brooklyn Promenade** in Brooklyn Heights. If you're feeling invigorated, walk back into Manhattan over the Brooklyn Bridge.

Stroll down **Park Avenue** and see the endless row of lit Christmas trees under a fresh cover of powder.

If the bustle of holiday shoppers starts to lose its cheer, head over to the **Garden Café at MoMA,** 11 W. 53rd St. [5th/6th] 708-9400, where you can watch the snow collect on sculptures by Picasso and Maillol.

For more solitude, try the **General Theological Seminary,** 175 Ninth Ave. [20th/21st] 243-5150. It's only open for a few hours Monday through Saturday, so call ahead. When you get there, prepare yourself for a wonderful respite as the snow falls inside the grounds of this hidden spot in the city.

Any excuse will do for a walk along **Hudson River Park.** Snow is an excellent one. You can watch nature interact with the twin towers, walk along the river, and look out to the Statue of Liberty.

There are plenty of places in the city with a fireplace (see entry on fireplaces). When it snows, though, we want to be dining at **I Trulli,** 122 E. 27th St. [Lexington/Park Ave. S.] 481-7372. Not only is the Apulian food good, there's a glassed-in fireplace, and you can watch the snow come down onto their terrace.

The **7 train from Times Square to Flushing** is our favorite subway line. Hop on when the snow starts and get elevated views of Manhattan. Hop off at almost any stop and you're sure to find excellent and authentic ethnic fare from one of dozens of countries. Then you get the ride home.

Thanksgiving Day Parade

*T*HE GIRAFFE WAS TOO TALL and some of the other animals behaved badly.

The first **Macy's Thanksgiving Day Parade** was in 1924 with a long route that started at 145th and Convent to 34th St. They borrowed some animals from the Central Park Zoo to liven things up. The giraffe had to stay home because it wouldn't fit under the elevated tracks. After the first couple of parades, when it became apparent that the animals weren't as kid-friendly as they might have liked, Macy's asked theatrical designer, Tony Sarg, to come up with some animal-shaped balloons. Felix the Cat, one of the first, was made at the Goodyear Tire company in Akron, Ohio, in 1927. A version of Felix is still parading.

For a few years the balloons were released after the parade and anyone who found one was entitled to a reward from Macy's. But this was stopped in 1933 after a student pilot stalled her engine over Jamaica Bay trying to snag a cat balloon and two tugboats in the East River tore the dachshund balloon apart. By 1934, Walt Disney characters such as

Mickey Mouse and Pluto joined the parade. During World War II, the rubber balloons were donated to the war effort and the parade didn't resume until 1947. It then began to develop as we know it: floats, celebrities, bigger and better balloons, coast-to-coast TV coverage, and store employees trained in the clown arts.

Popeye, Bullwinkle, and the 40 parade balloons begin to be inflated about 5 P.M. the day before the parade on 77th and 81st Streets between Central Park West and Columbus. The Parade steps off at 9 A.M. Thanksgiving Day morning at W. 77th St. and Central Park West. It marches south on Central Park West to Columbus Circle, around to Broadway, then down Broadway to Herald Square. It heads west on 34th St. and breaks up at Seventh Ave. Macy's Holiday Hotline is 494-4495.

Toys

℣EDDY BEARS, tea sets, marbles, and the hottest toys of the season:

B. Shackman & Co., 85 Fifth Ave. [16th] 989-5162. Miniatures for the doll house, tiny china tea sets for doll tea parties, paper cutouts, and many seasonal novelties and decorations . . .**Bear Hugs and Baby Dolls,** 311 E. 81st St. [1st/2nd] 717-1514. Dolls from a rare Cabbage Patch to Madame Alexander and a couple of hundred teddy bears. . .**A Bear's Place,** 789 Lexington Ave. [61st/62nd] 826-6465. Small versions of upholstered furniture among the bears and brightly colored pull toys. . .**Children's Museum of Manhattan,** 212 W. 83rd St. [Amsterdam/Broadway] 721-1234. The gift shop carries a well selected group of art, music, and imaginative toys. . .**Classic Toys,** 218 Sullivan St. [Bleecker/W.3rd] 674-4434, is devoted to toy soldiers and tiny cars and airplanes. . . **Dinosaur Hill,** 302 E. 9th St. [1st/2nd] 473-5850, has a nice selection of toys, hand puppets and marionettes, and glass marbles, as well as many dinosaurs. . .**The Enchanted Forest,** 85 Mercer St. [Spring/Broome] 925-6677. Creative and artistic toys with many stuffed animals and teddy bears, some of which are handmade by artists like Irene Heckel and Myrna and Bert Seva. . .**F.A.O. Schwarz,** 767 Fifth Ave. [58th] 644-9400. For many, the ultimate New York toy store.

Great American Teddy Bear, 538 Madison Ave. [54th/55th] 688-9394. The local outpost of the Vermont Teddy Bear Company sells the multicostumed critters. . .**Jan's Hobby Shop,** 1557 York Ave. [82nd/83rd] 861-5075, sells model kits for the young builder as well as the tools and paints you need to put them together. . .**Kidding Around,** 60 W. 15th St. [5th/6th] 645-6337. Toys are arranged by category: music, art, infant. Wide aisles and great variety make it a pleasant place to shop. . .**Little Extras,** 550 Amsterdam Ave. [86th/87th] 721-6161. Lots of scaled down tables and chairs, including an Adirondack lounge chair. . .**Little Rickie,** 49 ½ First Ave. [3rd] 505-6467. Elvis refrigerator magnets, glow-in-the-dark skeleton key chains, kitsch heaven for kids and adults—mostly adults. . .**Penny Whistle Toys,** 448 Columbus Ave. [81st/82nd] 873-9090, and 1283 Madison Ave. [91st/92nd] 369-3868. Many educational toys and nice stocking stuffers. . .**Red Caboose,** 23 W. 45th St. [5th/6th] 575-0155. For model trains, there's nothing like it in the city. . . **Star Magic,** 275 Amsterdam Ave. [73rd] 769-2020, 745 Broadway [8th] 228-7770 and 1256 Lexington Ave. [85th] 988-0300. New Age and science-related toys. . .**Tiny Doll House,** 1146 Lexington Ave. [79th/80th] 744-3719. Everything, including the kitchen sink, in miniature scale. . .**Uncle Futz,** 408 Amsterdam Ave. [79th/80th] 799-6723. Reliable sources for gifts from infant to pre-teen. . .**West Side Kids,** 498 Amsterdam Ave. [84th/85th] 496-7282. Tiny kitchen appliances and construction toys, including Erector sets.

Trains

$\mathcal{F}$OR MANY YEARS, Clarke Dunham carried an image around in his head of a large locomotive passing overhead on a high bridge.

One day he realized that the perspective was one of a small child looking up and that he was the child: the image was of himself, age three, at the 1939 World's Fair, gazing up at a model train. Fitting, then, that Mr. Dunham with his wife, Barbara, are the designers of the model train spectacular, "a stage set with trains," installed in the *Citicorp Building,* Lexington and 53rd Street 559-6758. It takes you on an imaginary trip from the meticulously re-created Weehawken, N.J., train station up the Hudson to the Catskills, ending in a snow scene. Tiny animated people saw wood, climb trees, or run a bulldozer amidst the changing scenery. The position of the 3-year-old viewer has been kept in mind by the designers: "It's designed for adults and children—there are always two eye levels, the lowest one being two feet above ground. Kids don't have to be picked up to see it." Mr. Dunham used his experience as a theatrical set designer in creating the magic and solving the technical problems. Trains cunningly appear and disappear while climbing a cleverly designed helical track around a mountain. Using trains in three scales, with the smallest at the top, forces the perspective and adds to the magic. "The higher you go, the more real it gets." The bridge that Mr. Dunham remembered for all those years has been re-created as well. It's on display from the Friday after Thanksgiving until the end of December. Admission is free.

Whether you like trains or not, you'll enjoy the *Holiday Garden Railways* that makes a stop at the New York Botanical Garden, Southern Blvd. and 200th St. Bronx 718-817-8700. This is the creation of Paul Busse, a landscape architect and model train enthusiast. Seven large model trains run on, over, around, and through mountains, forests, castles, moats, waterfalls, bridges, and tunnels. Models of New York City historic houses are created out of dried plant material. Edgar Allan Poe's house has a tiny twisted twig handrail and the uprights of the Brooklyn Bridge are maple bark. The effect, says Mr. Busse is of "the textures and the details of the buildings as you remember them, not as they actually are." The Botanical Garden Christmas tree is the centerpiece of the display. Admission charge with some free days.

Trees – Part 1

CHRISTMAS IN NEW YORK STARTS when they throw the switch on the 26,000 lights of the *Rockefeller Center Christmas Tree.*

The tradition of the tree started in 1931 when the construction workers building Rockefeller Center put up a small tree on the site. In 1933, an official tree, festooned with 700 blue and white lights, marked the holiday season and has ever since. It frequently comes from upstate but also has come from as far as Ottawa and is usually a Norway spruce between seventy-five and ninety feet tall. Once the tree is selected, it is suspended from the tip of a giant crane and laid on a trailer truck to begin its trip in the middle of the night, complete with police escort, into New York. The first televised lighting was in 1951 on Kate Smith's show. Now, the annual ceremony is generally the first Tuesday in December, in the early evening. 632-3975.

The fun of seeing the tree at the *American Museum of Natural History* is in picking out and identifying the origami animals. Over 1,000 constructions of everything from elephants and gorillas to dinosaurs, jellyfish, and beetles, can be seen from Thanksgiving till after New Year's Day. At a table nearby, volunteers teach simple origami folds to children. (Note: This tree may not be displayed while the new Biodiversity Halls are under construction.) 769-5100.

At the ***Forbes Magazine Galleries,*** 60 Fifth Ave. [11th/12th] 206-5548, they display as many as three Christmas trees. The 'political' tree has historical political ornaments dating back to the Victorian era. The 'Victorian antique' tree has other ornaments from that period, and there is, perhaps not surprisingly, a 'hot air balloon tree.'

The ***Lincoln Center*** tree sits in the Fountain Plaza and is ornamented with over 70 large musical instruments, ballet slippers and theatrical masks. Trees in the plaza have starburst lights based on the ones in the Met. The lighting ceremony takes place in the first week of December. There are carols, and Sesame Street characters mingle with kids. Cookies and cider for all. 546-2656.

Trees – Part 2

The Metropolitan Museum of Art places its tree in front of the eighteenth-century Spanish choir screen, which came from the Cathedral of Valladolid. It is decorated with a collection of eighteenth-century Neapolitan angels hovering over the 200 figures that make up the crèche at its base. There are lighting ceremonies on Friday and Saturday evenings. 535-7710.

The New York Stock Exchange tree, opposite the 18 Broad St. [Exchange/Wall] entrance, goes up Thanksgiving weekend and is lit the following Monday in a public ceremony with a choir. It's the second largest tree after Rockefeller Center (generally over sixty-five feet tall) with 10,000 lights. It is surrounded by four thirteen- and one-half-foot-tall toy soldiers and a ten-foot drum.

On *Park Avenue,* 20 foot evergreens are placed in the gardens from 54th to 96th Sts. for Christmas, and white lights are wound around cherry trees for Hanukkah. The tree lighting ceremony takes place on the first Sunday in December. Teams of electricians start at each end of the display and turn on the lights block by block while residents cheer them on from their windows. The Park Avenue trees went up for the first time in December, 1945 as a memorial to all in New York City who gave their lives in World War II. A ceremony at the **Brick Presbyterian Church,** Park Ave. and 91st St. 876-3322, rededicates the trees each year, now to all those who have sacrificed their lives for this country. The children's choir sings and the U.S. Army Band plays.

The South Street Seaport Museum follows the sea-going tradition of placing lit Christmas trees on the top of the masts of the six ships berthed there.

Other trees: There is a tree in front of **City Hall** and a ceremony, as well as a menorah lighting. A tree stands in the plaza of the **State Office Building in Harlem. Washington Square Park** has a Christmas tree lighting a couple of weeks before Christmas with caroling, near the arch.

Trimmings

$\mathcal{Y}$OU CAN FIND almost every holiday trimming imaginable at one of the following stores:

ABC Carpet and Home, 888 Broadway [19th] 473-3000, for ornaments made from glass beads, carved wood, and tiny hand-knit stockings.

Authentiques, 255 W. 18th St. [7th/8th] 675-2179, is a haven for printed drinking glasses, but at Christmas they display antique glass tree ornaments.

Henri Bendel's Ornament Shop, 712 Fifth Ave. [55th/56th] 247-1100, always stocks a good selection of holiday items.

Cathedral of St. John the Divine, Amsterdam and 112th St. 222-7200. The gift shop, located off the left side of the nave, is full of Advent calendars, angels, and much else.

Felissimo, 10 W. 56th St. [5th/6th] 247-5656, for a finely chosen assortment of holiday decorations.

The Gazebo, 114 E. 57th St. [Park/Lexington] 832-7077, for many handmade ornaments, but especially for the soft sculpture ornaments designed by Gladys Boalt. Representing historical figures from Vermeer to Benjamin

Franklin and the figures from children's stories like *The Nutcracker*, they are delightful.

The Incredible Christmas Store, Trump Tower, 725 Fifth Ave. [56th/57th] 754-1200. Open year-round selling all kinds of ornaments and holiday decorations from simple to high end.

Both ***James A. Cole,*** 41 W. 25th St. [6th/Broadway] 741-1500, and ***Kurt Adler's Santa's World,*** 1107 Broadway [24th/25th] 924-0900, open their otherwise "to the trade only" doors to the public after Thanksgiving. Lights, ornaments, garlands, and trims galore.

Kate's Paperie, 561 Broadway, [Prince] 941-9816, and 8 W. 13th St. [5th/6th] 633-0570, has unique, handmade items often imported just for them.

Macy's, Herald Square, 695-4400, has the largest selection of Christmas decorations in the city.

La Maison Moderne, 144 W. 19th St. [6th/7th] 691-9603, is a good source for small home decor items. At the holidays, that includes their velvet Christmas tree skirts.

Matt McGhee, 22 Christopher St. [Greenwich/Waverly] 741-3138. Ornaments of every imaginable shape, size, and price including many German hand-blown and hand-painted ones. We doubt you'll leave empty-handed.

Smith & Hawken, 394 W. Broadway [Spring/Broome] 925-0687, carries fruit- and vegetable-shaped glass ornaments and unusual garlands.

Tubas

TUBAS— A HAPPY CHRISTMAS TRADITION, and a wonderful story.

It is 1974, and Harvey Phillips is looking for a way to honor his tuba teacher, William Bell. Mr. Bell played with Sousa and Toscanini, and taught at Juilliard, but, Mr. Phillips thinks, he isn't well known to other tubists. In general, he discovers, tubists don't know other tubists. He sends letters to 400 tuba players around the country and asks if they would like to be part of a Christmas concert. Responses start to come in and now Mr. Phillips has to find a venue.

He says, "I thought New York would be a good place to have the concert because William Bell had taught there. I called Rockefeller Center and asked to speak to the vice president of public relations. I asked him if they ever used a stage behind the ice skating rink for concerts. He said this had never been done, but he asked, 'What kind of ensemble do you have?' I said, I don't have one but I expect around 300 tubas.' There was silence on the other end of the phone and he repeated his question." Sensing that the concept of 300 tubas isn't doing the trick, he tells the man from Rockefeller Center, "I'll give you the unlisted telephone numbers of some of my friends so you can check on me." An hour later, Mr. Phillips gets a phone call back saying, "I've spoken to your friends and you can have anything you want." The man from Rockefeller Center had just spoken with Leonard Bernstein, Morton Gould, Leopold Stokowski, Gunther Schuller, and Andre Kostelanetz.

There were no arrangements for 300 tubas, so Mr. Phillips asked Alec Wilder to do them, who, after a certain (perhaps understandable) reluctance, came up with 33. The first rehearsal was held on the second floor of the NBC building in a long corridor about twenty feet wide and eighty feet long. In addition to the musicians and Mr. Wilder, a group of friends, family, and reporters gathered there. After the cacophonous warmup, the conductor, Paul Lavalle, called for silence. Then 300 tubas began to play "O, Come All Ye Faithful." Mr. Phillips says, "Everyone began to cry and Alec Wilder was jumping up and down, hugging me, tears in his eyes, saying 'It works! It works!'"

Now, *Tuba Christmas* has 500 tubists and takes place annually on the second Sunday before Christmas at the ice rink in Rockefeller Plaza as well as in 155 other cities in the United States. Mr. Phillips says 150 or so of the 500 performers are under the age of 20, and some are 9 or 10 years old. "Can you imagine what it means to a ten-year-old who plays the tuba to find himself in a group containing symphony orchestra players?"

If you are interested in performing write to: Tuba Christmas, P.O. Box 933, Bloomington, IN 47402-0933. Tuba Christmas info: 332-6868.

'Twas the Night Before Christmas

SURELY APOCRYPHAL BUT CHARMING is one version of how Clement Clarke Moore came to write "A Visit from St. Nicholas." It is December 24th, 1822 and the Moore family needs their Christmas turkey. Mr. Moore leaves his Chelsea home via sleigh and pulls up to the Washington Market. En route, he has had the idea for the poem and starts composing on the way back. Later that evening, turkey dispatched and stockings hung, Mr. Moore recites the poem to his six children. The poem is published, unsigned, the next year in the *Troy Sentinel* (N.Y.), December 23rd, 1823, and becomes an immediate hit. It is then widely reprinted but not publicly attributed to, or admitted by, Moore until the publication of *The New York Book of Poetry* in 1837, a collection of verse by native-born New Yorkers. In 1848, it is published independently, illustrated with woodcuts by local artist Theodore C. Boyd. Some 40 years after he wrote the poem, Mr. Moore says his inspiration came during the sleigh ride. Okay by us, C. C.

'TWAS THE NIGHT BEFORE CHRISTMAS, when all through the house
Not a creature was stirring, not even a mouse;
The stockings were hung by the chimney with care,
In hopes that ST. NICHOLAS soon would be there;

The children were nestled all snug in their beds,
While visions of sugar-plums danced in their heads;
And mamma in her 'kerchief, and I in my cap,
Had just settled down for a long winter's nap,
When out on the lawn there arose such a clatter,
I sprang from the bed to see what was the matter.
Away to the window I flew like a flash,
Tore open the shutters and threw up the sash.
The moon on the breast of the new-fallen snow
Gave the lustre of mid-day to objects below,
When, what to my wondering eyes should appear,
But a miniature sleigh, and eight tiny reindeer,
With a little old driver, so lively and quick,
I knew in a moment it must be St. Nick.
More rapid than eagles his coursers they came,
And he whistled, and shouted, and called them by name;
"Now, DASHER! now, DANCER! now, PRANCER
    and VIXEN!
On, COMET! on CUPID! on, DONDER and BLITZEN!
To the top of the porch! to the top of the wall!
Now dash away! dash away! dash away all!"
As dry leaves that before the wild hurricane fly,
When they meet with an obstacle, mount to the sky,
So up to the house-top the coursers they flew,
With the sleigh full of toys, and St. Nicholas too.
And then, in a twinkling, I heard on the roof
The prancing and pawing of each little hoof.
As I drew in my hand, and was turning around,
Down the chimney St. Nicholas came with a bound.
He was dressed all in fur, from his head to his foot,
And his clothes were all tarnished with ashes and soot;
A bundle of toys he had flung on his back,
And he looked like a peddler just opening his pack.

His eyes—how they twinkled! his dimples how merry!
His cheeks were like roses, his nose like a cherry!
His droll little mouth was drawn up like a bow,
And the beard of his chin was as white as the snow;
The stump of a pipe he held tight in his teeth,
And the smoke it encircled his head like a wreath;
He had a broad face and a little round belly,
That shook when he laughed like a bowlful of jelly.
He was chubby and plump, a right jolly old elf,
And I laughed when I saw him, in spite of myself;
A wink of his eye and a twist of his head,
Soon gave me to know I had nothing to dread;
He spoke not a word, but went straight to his work,
And filled all the stockings; then turned with a jerk,
And laying his finger aside of his nose,
And giving a nod, up the chimney he rose;
He sprang to his sleigh, to his team gave a whistle,
And away they all flew like the down of a thistle.
But I heard him exclaim, ere he drove out of sight,
'HAPPY CHRISTMAS TO ALL, AND TO ALL
    A GOOD-NIGHT.'

Virginia

*I*T WAS 100 YEARS AGO THAT *The New York Sun* fashioned its famous editorial reply, "Yes, Virginia, There Is a Santa Claus," to Virginia O'Hanlon of 115 W. 95th Street.

Ms. O'Hanlon, who died in 1971, seems to have suffered no ill effects from the editorial: she earned her Ph.D. and went on to a long career as a teacher and administrator in the New York City school system. As we re-read it, stripping away our own scepticism in a sceptical age, we find the response most appealing.

> *The Sun* wrote: We take pleasure in answering thus prominently the communication below, expressing at the same time our great gratification that its faithful author is numbered among the friends of *The Sun:*

> Dear Editor—
> I am 8 years old. Some of my little friends say there is no Santa Claus. Papa says if you see it in *The Sun*, it's so. Please tell me the truth, is there a Santa Claus?
>
> VIRGINIA O'HANLON

VIRGINIA, YOUR LITTLE FRIENDS ARE WRONG. They have been affected by the scepticism of a sceptical age. They do not believe except they see. They think that nothing can be which is not comprehensible by their little minds. All minds, Virginia, whether they be men's or children's, are little. In this great universe of ours, man is a mere insect, an ant, in his intellect as compared with the boundless world about him, as measured by the intelligence capable of grasping the whole of truth and knowledge.

Yes, Virginia, there is a Santa Claus. He exists as certainly as love and generosity and devotion exist, and you know that they abound and give to your life its highest beauty and joy. Alas! how dreary would be the world if there were no Santa Claus! It would be as dreary as if there were no Virginias. There would be no childlike faith then, no poetry, no romance to make tolerable this existence. We should have no enjoyment, except in sense and sight. The external light with which childhood fills the world would be extinguished.

Not believe in Santa Claus! You might as well not believe in fairies. You might get your papa to have men to watch in all the chimneys on Christmas eve to catch Santa Claus, but even if you did not see Santa Claus coming down, what would that prove? Nobody sees Santa Claus, but that is no sign that there is no Santa Claus. The most real things in the world are those that neither children nor men can see. Did you ever see fairies dancing on the lawn? Of course not, but that's no proof that they are not there. Nobody can conceive or imagine all the wonders there are unseen and unseeable in the world.

You tear apart the baby's rattle and see what makes the noise inside, but there is a veil covering the unseen world which not the strongest man, nor even the united strength of all the strongest men that ever lived, could tear apart. Only faith, poetry, love, romance, can push aside that curtain and view and picture the supernal beauty and glory beyond. Is it all real? Ah, Virginia, in all this world there is nothing else real and abiding.

No Santa Claus! Thank God! he lives and lives forever. A thousand years from now, Virginia, nay 10 times 10,000 years from now, he will continue to make glad the heart of childhood.

Walks and Tours

WHETHER YOU LIVE IN NEW YORK or are visiting for the holidays, taking one of these tours will give you a new perspective on the city.

Big Onion Walking Tours has toured the Jewish Lower East Side on December 25th since 1990. Traffic is stopped in the neighborhood as several hundred people participate. "We have 10 guides, all of them graduate students in history, on duty that day," says Seth Kamil, director of Big Onion. Among the sites they visit are the Eldridge St. Synagogue, now landmarked, and the old headquarters of the *Jewish Daily Forward*. 439-1090.

The Municipal Arts Society will take you to The Best Dressed Landmarks of the Holidays. This tour visits the most elaborately decorated buildings, lobbies, atriums, and vest-pocket parks along Fifth and Madison Aves. 935-3960.

Francis Morrone, an architectural historian, gives a tour of Rockefeller Center several times each year, with several scheduled during the holiday season. "There is always heightened interest in Rockefeller Center at Christmas time," he says. He discusses the original planning of the project, as well as its architecture and decoration while taking you through the complex of buildings and public spaces. 935-3960.

Radio City Music Hall, 1260 Ave. of the Americas [50th] 632-4041. Behind and in front of the scenes in New York's Art Deco showplace.

Joyce Gold, who teaches the history of Manhattan at the New School for Social Research and NYU, gives a walking tour in the financial district the weekend after Thanksgiving. Ms. Gold compares the Dutch and English colonial traditions while taking you through the street layout of early Manhattan. 242-5762.

Nina Kauder gives a once-a-month food-related tour of the city that lasts almost a full day. Sometimes she focuses on a neighborhood, sometimes on an item such as bread, cheese, or chocolate. 780-9771.

Heritage Trails New York, Federal Hall National Memorial, 26 Wall St. [Broad] 1-888-4-TRAILS, incorporates the contemporary decorations into their historical tours.

For those who have had enough of the holidays, **Radical Walking Tours** will take you around either Greenwich Village or the East Village, pointing out sites associated with Woody Guthrie, Emma Goldman, and the War Resister's League. 718-492-0069.

There are daily tours of the **Cathedral of St. John the Divine,** Amsterdam and 112th St. 316-7540. You can see the highlights of New York City's unfinished Gothic cathedral, its architecture, construction, the windows, tapestries and the cathedral's art collection.

Winter Solstice

S OME WAYS TO MARK THE LONGEST NIGHT OF THE
YEAR.

Musicians play from perches in the apses and chancels of the
Cathedral of St. John the Divine, Amsterdam and 112th St.,
during the Winter Solstice Celebration given each year by
Cathedral artist-in-residence, The Paul Winter Consort. A
stage erected in the middle of the center aisle is the focus for
the nearly 3,000 people who attend this metaphorical jour-
ney. Giant floats, one representing the Earth, are maneu-
vered around the cathedral accompanied by dancers and
singers. Mr. Winter makes each year's concert "as ecumeni-
cal as possible, in keeping with the cathedral and honors all
of the traditions that have a holiday in the December period.
Hanukkah, Christmas and Kwanzaa are all festivals of
renewal." Dancers, musicians, and singers from different
cultures perform separately as first, then come together in a
pulsing and exciting finale. Near the end of the concert, the
audience gets into the act with a full-throated wolf howl.
"The howling began in 1973 when I was interested in the
music in the voices of wolves. Originally, the Consort would

howl; now, the audience howls. It's a form of participation where you can go full tilt and be forceful. It's a liberating experience for people. And there are no wrong notes in a howl chorus." The end of each concert is signaled by a large golden sun gong in the far apse of the cathedral. Scott Sloan, a musician who also happens to be a high-wire rigger, sits in a bosun's chair next to the gong. Instrument and player slowly rise 100 feet to the ceiling of the cathedral, and the days become imperceptibly longer until June. Tickets required. 662-2133.

The purpose of ***The Christmas Revels at Symphony Space,*** 2537 Broadway [95th] 864-5400, is "to keep away the dark." Each year focuses on a particular tradition, French, perhaps, or Celtic or German, there is music and dancing and a mix of the pagan and the religious. The effect is of "typical village entertainment at that time of year." The audience gets a chance to sing and to join a line dance through the aisles. Six performances are given as near to the solstice as possible. Tickets required.

St. Mark's-in-the-Bowery Church, 131 E. 10th St. [Stuyvesant/3rd], presents its Winter Solstice performance at the exact time of the solstice. James Nyoraku Schlefer plays the Japanese bamboo flute called the shakuhachi. Mr. Schlefer gathers a dozen or so shakuhachi players and disposes them on two levels and around three sides of the church. Playing a combination of original and traditional music, "the natural acoustics of the building" and the haunting breathy sound of the flutes provide what many people have called a meditative experience. Free. 674-6377.

Wrapping It Up

*K**ate's Paperie,*** 561 Broadway [Prince/Spring] 941-9816, and 8 W. 13th St. [5th/6th] 633-0570, is where to go when you want to give your gifts and packages a special touch.

The "paper wall" runs the length of the Broadway store and shows off hundreds of papers from filmy laces to ones mimicking leather or metal. Papers that are embedded with flower petals, leaves, or glitter confetti, have crinkly or basket weave textures, patterned or iridescent surfaces come from just about every country in the world. Add to this over 30 colors of tissue paper and a selection of ribbons from string thin to hand span wide, gilded, printed, wired, and ombred. Red and green, too. A staff of trained wrappers at each location can help you come up with a good combination of supplies for a memorable gift presentation from the tailored to the extravagant.

Don't want to do it yourself? Kate's has a wrapping service which works like this: If you spend at least $10 on materials, a Kate's "basic wrap"—pleated paper on the front of the box (for long life, good luck and happiness) and a double ribbon in a cunning bow on top—is free. If you want a more complicated wrap—double papers, origami fans, or elaborate bows—prices are worked out on a per-project basis. If you buy a gift at Kate's, the basic wrap is on the house, using their paper of the day and a raffia tie.

Ron Raznick's company **RTR Packaging,** 27 W. 20th St. [5th/6th] 620-0011, generally provides papers and packaging for boutiques and cosmetic companies. But you can go there, too, for high-quality printed papers in wonderful colors in sheets or rolls, along with clever printed boxes that make a nice presentation without any additional fussing. RTR has wraps themed for Christmas, Hanukkah, and Kwanzaa packaging too.

Here's where we wrap up this book until next year. We hope you have a joyous holiday season and a Happy New Year.

Index

About the Authors

CHARLES A. SUISMAN and CAROL MOLESWORTH have published the newsletter *Manhattan User's Guide* since 1992, a discriminating resource guide for New Yorkers on the best shopping, restaurants, services, amusements, good deals, and resources in New York City.

In 1996, Hyperion published an updated collection of newsletter articles, also entitled *Manhattan User's Guide,* available in bookstores everywhere.

Microsoft's New York Sidewalk, http://newyork.sidewalk. com, features a weekly column from *Manhattan User's Guide* that answers New Yorkers' questions about the city.

For more information, call 212-724-4692 or email mugoffice@msn.com.

ABOUT THE ILLUSTRATOR

CHESLEY MCLAREN celebrates the beginning of the holidays with the Christmas Ride at Claremont Stables in Central Park. Chesley lives in New York.